The
Dirtiest
Little
Limerick
Book
Ever

The Dirtiest Little Limerick Book Ever

By Albin Chaplin

Bell Publishing Company
New York

This 1984 edition is published by Bell Publishing Company
by arrangement with Albin Chaplin.

Manufactured in the United States of America

ISBN: 0-517-433907

h   g   f   e   d   c   b   a

Designed by Brian Malloy

INTRODUCTION

This book contains more than 550 of my favorite dirty limericks, covering a wide range of subject matter and providing something for everyone. Some limericks are lecherous, some are grossly indecent, some are humorous, some are witty, and some may even be shocking, yet they are all designed to evoke a hearty laugh and to break down inhibitions at any gathering. Laughter is enjoyment and it is good therapy; people who smile can expect to live longer, and it has been noted that a sick person can actually laugh his way to good health.

The limerick may be vulgar, and indeed all the good ones are vulgar, but it is not really pornographic, since it produces laughter. A joke can produce the same result, but a limerick is better than a joke since it is good poetry and it has a special appeal for literate, word-oriented people. There is no question that the limerick has established itself as a form of folklore that never seems to lose its freshness. The limerick is easily memorized, and it can be repeated thousands of times without any loss of impact—I suspect that it even gains in potency with repetition. Seldom does a listener say, "I've heard that one before." Rather, he is more apt to remark, "Give it to me again." A good five-liner is somewhat like sex—repetition does not dull the desire to participate.

Writers on the subject agree that the appeal of the limerick emanates from the following characteristics: the concise story in five lines, the strict art form, the innocuous beginning, the rapid development, and the illogical insanity of the unexpected ending, which is often devastating in its effect. All this is supplied in the anapestic meter, which is without doubt one of the major characteristics that contribute to the unending fascination with the limerick. After all, have we not all been nurtured on the anapestic in "Twas the night before Christmas, when all through the house" and "The Assyrian came down like the wolf on the fold"? These poems are *so* easy to learn! Even Mozart used the anapestic in a memorable aria in *The Magic Flute.* The very popular dance form, the waltz, is anapestic, best exemplified by "The Blue Danube."

Perhaps in the near future some enterprising biologist will trace the infatuation with the limerick to a five-line anapestic gene located near, or attached to, the gene for sexual fulfillment. It is interesting to note that sexually repressed individuals dislike and even loathe the off-color joke or limerick, finding it offensive. Vulgarity is a distinctive feature of the limerick that adds immeasurably to its enjoyment, although there are some alleged enthusiasts who take the opposite viewpoint, saying that the clean limerick is the only limerick. There are no "good" words or "bad" words, for "good" and "bad" are simply moral judgments foisted upon society.

As G. Legman, a noted author of limericks, has observed, "A clean limerick has never been of the slightest real interest to anyone" and "The clean sort of limerick is an obvious palliation, its content insipid, its rhyming artificially ingenious, its whole permeated with a frustrated nonsense." Vulgarity does have its place, for it provides the shock therapy, breaks down taboos, and attacks the moral superficiality imposed upon society.

I trust that the items in this book will meet the high standards of good limericks—to be not too clean—and will provide the reader with many hours of relaxation, and perhaps in some small measure will contribute to the continued pleasure of social gatherings.

Sarasota, Florida   ALBIN CHAPLIN
1984

The
Dirtiest
Little
Limerick
Book
Ever

The limerick that has the appeal
Is penned by the quill that's facile
    In the sordid, grotesque,
    And in bawdy burlesque,
And contorted reports imbecile.

〜〜〜

All women would gain more affinity
With husbands who'd love to infinity,
    And wives' troubles would pass
    If they'd struggle for ass
Just as hard as they fought for virginity.

〜〜〜

When Hoover was dating Miss Beggs,
She said, when she spread out her legs,
    "I deplore, Mr. Hoover,
    Such a lengthy maneuver;
It is time for the sausage and eggs."

〜〜〜

TRY A DRY RUN!

A lady went out with young Bert
But he couldn't get under her skirt.
    He said, "Do you fear
    A prick?" She said, "Dear,
It isn't the prick—it's the squirt!"

〜〜〜

LISSAJOUS FIGURE

A jungle explorer named Biggar
Was fucking a colored gold digger.
    It was just like a tonic
    With her fanny harmonic
Which traced a fine Lissajous figure.

~~~~~~

A young sausage-stuffer, Miss Binks,
Stuffed sausage all day into links.
    Her nightly routine
    Was more sausage between,
And she never could catch forty winks.

~~~~~~

WHERE DID HE KISS HER?

There was a young fellow named Bister
Who fucked Miss Laporte and her sister.
    When he fucked Miss Laporte
    'Twas a marathon sport,
But her sister would come when he kissed her.

~~~~~~

QUIET PLEASE!

In the library, stuffy Miss Boyes
Was raped, but she maintained her poise.
    Though her arms waved about
    There was nary a shout—
She respected the rule against noise.

~~~~~~

A drowning old harlot named Clive
Was pulled from the lake half alive.
    On reviving she spoke
    She could not swim a stroke,
But she swore that she knew every dive.

~~~~~~

HATCHET MAN

The woodchopper dated Miss Brackett
And proceeded to take off his jacket.
    Her pussy felt tight
    But he said with smile bright,
He was sure without doubt he could hack it.

~~~~~~

In the sticks lives a lady named Bright
With a face that's a horrible fright,
    But no fellow minds that—
    She feeds gin to her cat—
And it's fun when her pussy is tight.

~~~~~~

THE CORRECT RECIPE

From the book a young lady named Brook
Was unable to learn how to cook,
    But to fuck she was able,
    So she lay on the table
And supported her ass with the book.

~~~~~~

ANY PORT IN A STORM

A stoical fellow named Bud
Was fucking a lady—a dud—
    And she had a bad smell,
    But he said, "What the hell,
It is better than pulling my pud."

~~~~~~

"Your price—is it firm?" said young Croft,
While fondling her ass in the loft.
    She said, "Why you worm,
    It's got to be firm;
It will never go in if it's soft."

~~~~~~

Said the lady to old butcher Carr,
"Your sausage is not up to par."
    But his sausage went in
    Till it tickled her chin,
Which was stretching a good thing too far.

A frustrated fellow named Chase
Had nothing to say to wife Grace
    For three decades or so—
    But his family did grow
For he only was mad at her face.

The mother of buxom Miss Claire
Discovered her secret affair.
    She admonished her child
    For her antics so wild,
"This is something we both have to share."

"See-through fashions are fun," said old Clark.
"They fill me with vigor and spark.
    It makes life with wife Claribel
    A little more bearable,
For I always get fucked in the dark."

While having with wifie coition
The hubby jumped up with cognition
    And he cried, "Oh my dear,
    I have hurt you I fear,
For I felt a slight change in position."

In need of a man, widow Cotter
Went to bed with a fellow named Potter.
    She was no good in bed
    So she said to him, "Fred,
You can finish the fuck with my daughter."

~~~~~

On going to college, Miss Dare
By mother was told to beware
    Of boys in her bed
    For this she did dread,
So Dare fucked the boys in a chair.

~~~~~

THE LAW OF GRAVITY
Young Newton partook of depravity
And filled up a young lady's cavity.
    To indulge in some brevity,
    What to Newton was levity
He found was a law of some gravity.

~~~~~

A lady had thought to discuss
With the driver, her rape on the bus,
    Till she noticed the sign
    Which said ten dollar fine
If you raise on the bus any fuss.

~~~~~

A man who made Mary in Dover
Had Mercy when out in the clover.
    With Joy he did jump
    Then with Ethyl did pump,
And of course, he felt Rosie all over.

~~~~~

While checking the cunt of Miss Drew,
The doctor tried one inch, then two.
Said Miss Drew, without merriment,
"Please forget the experiment—
You can shove in the prick and let's screw."

~~~~~

The snatch of the Countess Dumore
Was bald as the knob on the door.
Said the Duke, in surprise,
As he parted her thighs,
"No doubt it's because of the war."

~~~~~

A man with his pecker erected
To fondle his dear wife elected.
With her clit he did play
But he found in dismay
That her pussy was not well connected.

~~~~~

VAGINA DENTATA
Said a girl to a lad, "You excite me.
Your prick in my cunt would delight me."
Said the novice young lad,
"I'll not do it, by Gad,
For I fear it will come back to bite me."

~~~~~

EASY DOES IT
To the doc said the heart patient, Fife,
"Will intercourse shorten my life?"
"Not a bit," said the doc,
"You will suffer no shock
Just as long as you fuck with the wife."

~~~~~

6

A young lady investor, Miss Finches,
Was observing the oil rigs and winches.
     She said, "Though it is fun
     To see deep drilling done,
I am thrilled if I'm drilled for six inches."

~~~~~

A wavy-haired lady named Flavey
Got more out of screwing than Davy,
     For when fucking was done
     She received half the fun,
And besides, she got all of the gravy.

~~~~~

ASTRONOMY CLASS

The astronomer asked young Miss Ford
If she ever the stars had explored.
     She replied, "In the night
     I see stars clear and bright
When I lay on my back and I'm bored."

~~~~~

A young coed freshman named Fretter
In fucking could not earn a letter,
     But when she was a soph
     She worked under a prof
And got better and better and better.

~~~~~

Epileptic cornhusker, young Fritz
Shucked corn and he shucked between fits.
     He dated Miss Bruce
     Whose bowels were loose,
So he fucked in between fits and shits.

~~~~~

The landlady, kind, gentle-hearted,
Would wait till her husband departed,
　　Then she'd treat her new roomer
　　With a peak 'neath her bloomer,
Which explains how the roomer got started.

The wife of a young man named Goozie
Had left him a little bit woozy.
　　In the place of resisting
　　She attempted assisting,
And he thought he was back with his floozie.

A soft-hearted lady named Gore
Gave the G.I.'s relief from the war.
　　But the anxious Marines
　　Could not get in her jeans—
She was rotten, they said, to the corps.

On a date with a lady, young Gore
At first thought his girl was a bore
　　For her mother had said
　　Don't take boys into bed,
But she fucked very well on the floor.

A homely old lady named Grace
Had plenty of dates at her place.
　　She was classed as first rate
　　For she'd greet a new date
With her dress pulled up over her face.

SMALL WORLD

There was a young fellow named Hame
Whose wife her great love did proclaim.
When his plant moved to Rome
There he built a new home,
But his milkman, he found, was the same.

~~~~~~

Said a frustrated bride, Mrs. Hayes,
"Education on sex matters pays,
For my groom, so untaught,
Cannot locate my twat,
And he's asked for a couple more days."

~~~~~~

The wife of a fellow named Hite
Said the headache she had was a fright.
But he said, with some thought,
"You can spread out your twat—
In your head I won't fuck you tonight."

~~~~~~

RICH FOOD

A lady who found herself huffing
Observed that her belly was puffing.
It was due to the gravy
Of a cook in the navy,
And the sausage and eggs and the stuffing.

~~~~~~

Ingenious indeed was young Hugh;
His girl also cleverness knew.
For a ride they did go
And had three in a row
On a bicycle fashioned for two.

~~~~~~

An expedient young fellow was Hugh;
In church he knew just what to do.
>   While the priest was exhorting
>   On immoral cavorting
He was fucking a nun in the pew.

～～～

From his wife, a young fellow named Jack
Got much more than a fair share of flak.
>   So he said, "You know what,
>   If it weren't for your twat
I would leave you and never come back."

～～～

THE FICKLE FINGER

A naive young lady named Kate
Requested a drink from her date:
>   "Just two fingers for me."
>   But he poured her full three.
She was Fucked by the Finger of Fate!

～～～

SOLOMON'S CHOICE

Old women, said learned Judge Kett,
For him were the very best bet.
>   They won't yell, tell or swell,
>   And they fuck hard as hell,
For it may be the last one they'll get!

～～～

A thorough young thief named Lautrec
Once frisked an old maid from Quebec.
>   He discovered no money
>   But she said to him, "Honey,
Don't stop now, I will write you a check."

～～～

The intelligent newlyweds, Lee,
Sensed the future had no guarantee.
    They faced life, but on guard;
    They both knew 'twould be hard,
But they knew not how long it would be.

~~~~~

FIVE MORE TO GO

She screamed with great joy as young Lynch
Provided the meat in the clinch.
    She cried, "God, but you're great!"
    But he said to her, "Kate,
You have only received the first inch."

~~~~~

While out with his girl, young MacBird
Some feelings erotic bestirred.
    With boldness and pluck
    He asked, "Do you fuck?"
She said, "Yes, but please don't use that word."

~~~~~

There was a young girl of Madras
Whose marriage was as fragile as glass,
    For her husband, sweet dove,
    Needed plenty of love,
But this bitch had a hunger for ass.

~~~~~

To her husband, old Mrs. Magoo
Said, "I'm beat and too tired to screw."
    Said her husband, discreet,
    "While I stick in the meat
Please lay still like you usually do."

~~~~~

11

A popular lady was Marge;
Her number of suitors was large.
    One young caller polite
    Said, "Are you free tonight?"
She said, "Darling, you know I don't charge."

~~~~~~

A dentist by name of McGavity
Was subject to fits of depravity.
    On his chair sat a maid
    And her teeth she displayed,
But he probed and he filled the wrong cavity.

~~~~~~

Though the nations all feared Caesar's name,
Not just war, but in love he won fame.
    Said the Queen of the Nile,
    "I admired his style,
For he saw and he conquered and came."

~~~~~~

A lady with hot pants in Oregon
Was screwed by a fellow named Corrigan.
    She had four on the floor
    But she wanted some more
So he fucked her four more on the floor again.

~~~~~~

An African hunter named Pace
Felt the need of a female embrace,
    So he looked for a cutie
    And he found him a beauty
With horseshit and flies on her face.

~~~~~~

GAME FELLOW

An African hunter named Pete
Would often play *Lion* with his sweet.
    He requested she prowl
    On her knees, with a growl,
Then proceeded to throw her the meat.

～～～

There was a young man of Purdue
Who bragged of the women he slew,
    But a nymph from De Witt
    Forced this man to admit,
"One more victory like this and I'm through."

～～～

A bachelor fellow named Ramon
Would check before letting a dame in.
    Of a girl, he asked, "Mary,
    Do you still have your cherry?"
She said, "No, just the box that it came in."

～～～

The psychiatrist heard with reflection
While a maid gave her tale of dejection.
    He leaned back with a sigh
    As he unzipped his fly
And he slipped her some love and affection.

～～～

"My honeymoon," young Stover said,
"Will last and with passion be fed."
    But you'll find, Mr. Stover,
    That the honeymoon's over
When the bride lets her first fart in bed.

～～～

A prudent young fellow named Sam
Was screwing a girl from Siam.
    He said to her, "Nellie,
    If you don't use some jelly
I am sure you will be in a jam."

~~~~~~

There was a young lady named Schilling
Who said to the oil man, "I'm willing
    To engage your fine rig,
    But it looks mighty big
So forget any off-the-shore drilling."

~~~~~~

An ugly old maid was Miss Schmidt,
As homely as two crocks of shit,
    But her boyfriend was simple
    For he loved every pimple
And he prized every wart on her tit.

~~~~~~

The housewife her duty does shirk
As she jumps into bed with a smirk
    And she shows her crevasse,
    But she parcels her ass
In return for some specified work.

~~~~~~

OR WAS IT A WEINER?
The butcher was fucking Miss Shore
Who lay on the butcher shop floor.
    She pondered the ceiling
    And had a strange feeling
She had felt that salami before.

~~~~~~

The fellow that fucked Lady Smith
Said, "You are great fun to be with;
    By the way, I am Thor."
    She said, "Me too—no more—
I'm tho thore that I hardly can pith."

≈≈≈≈

"With my wife I'm fed up," said old Snyder.
"As a bride she was fun when astride her.
    At first, I admit,
    There was a small split,
But at present the split is much wider."

≈≈≈≈

The housewife exposed her breasts so
She would set the old plumber aglow.
    Said the plumber at that,
    "I've no time to chew fat,
I have time just to come and to go."

≈≈≈≈

There was a young sparrow with spark
Who flew to the park in the dark.
    He came back to the nest,
    Kissed his mate and confessed
That he only went off on a lark.

≈≈≈≈

When a man placed his hand on her thigh,
The young lady remarked with a sigh,
    "You cannot have my heart."
    Said the man, "We must part,
For I did not aspire that high."

≈≈≈≈

A lively young girl of Toronto
Was harder than hell to hold on to.
    It required the Lone Ranger
    With his horse and a stranger
To restrain her while fucking old Tonto.

~~~~~

In his sled Santa placed every toy,
But this action was only a ploy
    To mislead Mrs. Claus,
    And his reason—because
He was spending the night spreading Joy.

~~~~~

Young Ivan watched Anne on the tractor
And took off his pants to distractor.
    Her position to Ivan
    Suggested connivin',
So he climbed on the tractor and factor.

~~~~~

Young lads will resort to strange tricks
To jump in the hay with young chicks.
    Even old ones will do,
    Be they black, brown or blue,
For no conscience is found in stiff pricks.

~~~~~

The young man who was dating Miss Venus
Had some trouble erecting his penis,
    So with candor, she said,
    As she climbed into bed,
"Let's get something, my dear, straight between us."

~~~~~

The lady next door got the votes
Of a family of goatherds named Coates,
    For she fucked with them all,
    The great grandfather tall,
And the father, the son and the goats.

There was a young fellow named Wilford
Who married a lady of Milford.
    They were married in June,
    Not a moment too soon,
For the mass of her ass had been pilfered.

EMISSION PROBLEM

An engine mechanic Alphonse
Looked ruefully down at his schwantz,
    For it pained when he piddled
    And it kinked when he diddled
And was lacking a motor response.

The crotch of a harlot Alsatian
Was largest throughout the whole nation,
    But she said the enormity
    Of her grievous deformity
Was the hazard of her occupation.

An old man with two pricks, from Azores,
Had one small and one big as a boar's.
    His dear wife he would stick
    With his undersize prick,
But the big was for bitches and whores.

At the circus, a stunt girl Miss Barr
Displayed antics that made her a star,
    But her ride on two horses
    Heading opposite courses—
It was stretching a good thing too far.

~~~~~~

To her husband, a lady named Blaining
Of his shortness of prick was complaining.
    But he said to her, "Dear,
    It's your pussy, I fear,
For it looks like a ditch used for draining."

~~~~~~

In the cunt of a girl named Cahalan
You could insert a broom and a pail in.
    Said her husband, "We're through."
    And he married anew
To a girl with a space for a whale in.

~~~~~~

A world-circling pussy cartel
Composed of Dupont, Ford and Shell,
    Proposed close control
    As their primary goal,
So a poor man could not get a smell.

~~~~~~

A newlywed man raised a clamor,
For nude, his new bride had no glamor,
    But she countered, "You simp,
    You're revoltingly limp;
It's like driving a worm with a hammer."

~~~~~~

A whore spent three months in confinement,
Her cunt was way out of alignment,
    And the doc did admit
    He could not help a bit,
So she peddled her ass on consignment.

~~~~

To bed went a baker of Crete
With a girl that he found on the street.
    "My God," said the baker,
    "This twat is an acre!"
So she offered her asshole petite.

~~~~

Cried the dumfounded groom in despair,
"My pecker will never fit there!"
    But his bride countered, "Hell,
    It should fit very well,
And with plenty left over to spare."

~~~~

Though she hadn't the tenth of a dollar,
An old harlot for taxis did holler.
    She tried raising her skirt
    And a cab did alert,
But he asked if she had something smaller.

~~~~

The cunt doctor looks and he feels
And ponders each crotch as he kneels,
    Then he writes so obscure
    A prescription for cure,
But it seems that the wound never heals.

~~~~

The Duchess of York never flinches
When the king pats her ass and he pinches,
For she welcomes a date
From the head of the state;
Every ruler, she knows, has twelve inches.

～～～～

THE REALIST
When Rosie was dating young Fritz,
Her father was pleased, he admits.
He said, "Fritz, you are grand,
Would you care for her hand?"
Fritz said, "No, just her cunt and her tits."

～～～～

A rapist deflowered Miss Grace
And the jury was trying the case.
Said His Honor, Judge Beggs,
"You may spread out your legs;
I must see where this foul act took place."

～～～～

There was a young lady named Gubb
Whose cunt was as big as a tub.
There was room for her groom
And a mop and a broom,
And some space for an evergreen shrub.

～～～～

There was a young barmaid named Gwen
With a cunt like the canyon called "Glen."
She was fucked on a date
And the man blew at eight,
And the echo was heard around ten.

～～～～

An old engineer name of Hector
Had a prick with a built-in corrector,
To correct for the mass
And the heat of the ass
And the bore and the stroke and the vector.

~~~~~

The crotch of a girl named Hilaria
Was largest in all of Bavaria.
Said old Baron von Bliss,
"Der dimension, vot iss?"
"Do you want," she said, "volume or area?"

~~~~~

"Let's go to see *Jaws*," said Miss Hunt,
"A show about sharks that is blunt."
Said her man, graciously,
"I would much rather see
The jaws that you find in a cunt."

~~~~~

THE NEW MATH
A teacher of math named Miss Hunt
Developed a fine teaching stunt.
She would clear up distractions
And explain vulgar fractions
By exposing a fraction of cunt.

~~~~~

A ROSE IS A ROSE IS A ROSE
An explorer of note once did hunt
Through the masses of hair out in front
Of Miss Stein's crotch hirsute,
And observed, so astute
That a cunt is a cunt is a cunt.

~~~~~

There was a magician named Jack
Whose prick had an uncommon knack.
    He could fit any cunt,
    Whether fat, tall or runt,
And change color to suit white or black.

~~~~~~

A near-sighted fellow named Juba
Was playing a piece on his tuba,
    When across on the floor
    Without pants walked a whore,
"Say Fidel," he said, "why'd you leave Cuba?"

~~~~~~

A haggard old harlot named Keating
Encountered in life such a beating,
    She was buggered and worn
    And her asshole was torn
And her pussy was not fit for eating.

~~~~~~

There was a young lady of Kitchener
Who had a most terrible itch in her.
    A lad offered relief
    But he ran like a thief
When he saw the great size of the ditch in her.

~~~~~~

For screwing, a fellow of Leeds
No jelly could find for his needs,
    So he said, "What the damn,
    I'll try raspberry jam."
But his foreskin got jammed with the seeds.

~~~~~~

An overworked harlot was Lizzie
Who left a young man in a tizzy,
    For her pussy was bare
    And her answer was, "There
Is no grass on a street that is busy."

A cautious young fellow named Lumming
Selected young girls with good plumbing.
    He advised, "When I choose 'em
    They must have a big bosom
So I plug in and hear myself coming."

Said a floundering fellow named Manion,
As he fucked with his lady companion,
    "I've had better, I think,
    When I pulled on my dink
On a trip to the depths of Grand Canyon."

The girl of a lip-reader, Morse,
Said "No" as a matter of course.
    Said Morse to her, "Bess,
    Please raise up your dress.
I must hear from the mouth of the horse."

THE SAGA OF CORKSCREW DICK

A corkscrew-pricked fellow of Natchez
Tried thousands and thousands of snatches,
    But this fellow named Dick
    Found no cunt for his prick,
And he cried in despair, "Nothing matches!"

In France, a young lady named List
Had a cunt with a helical twist.
    She could not find a fit
    For her helical slit,
So she cried in remorse, "I am pissed!"

In the circus Miss List did enlist
Where she pissed with a spiraling twist.
    All the patrons convulsed
    But Miss List was repulsed,
For a fuck was the thing that she missed.

When Dick saw Miss List piss a twister,
He ran to the ring and he kissed her.
    Then he showed her his thing
    Which was coiled like a spring,
And she yelled to him, "Fuck me now, mister!"

They checked that their spirals turned right
And they faced their first fuck with delight.
    On Miss List Dick did flop
    And he spun like a top,
And their organs at last did unite.

Their screams of despair were symmetric,
And they needed assistance obstetric,
    For Dick's thread, you can guess,
    Was a standard U.S.,
But Miss List had a cunt that was metric.

Their ending was sad, we admit;
Their organs were shattered and split.
From the force that existed
Both their assholes were twisted
And they died amidst spirals of shit.

~~~

As the twisted old cock of Doc Perce
Was rammed in the cunt of his nurse,
She complained—but too late—
By a strange twist of fate
She had taken a turn for the worse.

~~~

A man who knew cheese to perfection
Was asked how he made his selection.
He answered, "By Jesus,
I sniff all the cheeses,
And I choose cheese which fosters erection."

~~~

An expert well-digger named Pflugge
Wed a girl with a cunt like a jug
For he noted the size
Of the hole in her thighs
Was the same as the last well he dug.

~~~

GOOD DEED FOR THE DAY
Much obliged was a lady named Pyle
When a Boy Scout assisted a while,
So she said, "In what way
Can I brighten your day?"
He said, "Flash me a vertical smile!"

~~~

The prick of a fellow named Schink
Was set in a teratoid kink,
    So he cut off the end
    Where it started to bend
And he used it for mixing his drink.

~~~~~~~

PIT STOP
Said a girl to a fruit-picker, Schmidt,
"A sweet cherry you'll find in my slit."
    Replied Schmidt, up her flue,
    "What you say may be true,
But I never have seen such a pit."

~~~~~~~

So big was the cunt of Miss Sears
That it thrilled a young man, it appears.
    In amazement he said,
    "May I stick in the head?"
She said, "Yes sir, but just to the ears."

~~~~~~~

The lady from China is sought
For sideways direction of twat,
    And the more that you spread her
    The more it gets better,
For it tightens the pussy a lot.

~~~~~~~

A salesgirl of perfume, Miss Tish,
Stunk bad, though her pussy she'd swish.
    Said her boss, "You must leave,
    But there's no need to grieve.
You can work as a monger of fish."

~~~~~~~

RECORD IN THE ROCKS

A noted geologist, Walt,
Once screwed a young lady of Galt.
    She said, "You are proficient,
    Is my fissure sufficient?"
But her fissure, he said, was a fault.

~~~~~~

There was a young girl from the West
With tits on the back of her chest.
    Though her face was a fright
    She had dates every night
Since for dancing by far she was best.

~~~~~~

On his back lay a fellow from Wheeling
While he fondled his cock with great feeling.
    On the knob of his cock
    Came a fly for a walk,
And he plastered the fly to the ceiling.

~~~~~~

A well-hung young fellow named Zeeter
Was blessed with a twelve-inch long peter.
    Said a lady, so thrilled,
    "Now my cunt will be filled!"
But young Zeeter proceeded to eat her.

~~~~~~

There was an explorer named Behring
Who spoke of his exploits so daring,
    "I've fucked ladies so vigorous
    That strong men found them rigorous,
And I've fucked them as dead as a herring."

~~~~~~

The agile contortionist Burgess
Said, "Dear, I've a new way to merge us."
    They contorted a knot
    Which was drawn up so taut
That the church bells are now tolling dirges.

~~~~~

A horny young fellow named Chuck
Was challenged to prove he had pluck,
    So in utter defiance
    Of the laws known to science,
He engaged with himself in a fuck.

~~~~~

On the street in a hurry walked Clyde,
And he noticed a whore by his side.
    When he said, "I can't stay."
    She replied, "If you pay,
I believe I can take this in stride."

~~~~~

A wealthy old harlot named Commer
Fell dead after fucking old Palmer.
    Though her will did declare
    The last fucker would share,
Palmer lost to the wily embalmer.

~~~~~

A dignified harlot of Dimmage
Would caution each man in the scrimmage
    There'd be less of a bind
    If they acted refined
So that no one would fuck up her image.

~~~~~

There was a canoeist named Ewing
Who took a young lady canoeing.
 She was playful and chipper
 As she unzipped his zipper;
This undoing canoeing meant screwing.

~~~~~~~

The Byrd brothers snared Sally Fern
And each of them raped her in turn,
 But they ran out of breath
 And she fucked them to death,
And she killed off two Byrds with one stern.

~~~~~~~

A LITTLE LIE WON'T HURT

The old woodcarver's helper, Miss Fry,
Took Pinocchio aside on the sly,
 Then she took off her clothes
 And she stuffed his big nose
In her cunt, and said, "Now tell a lie!"

~~~~~~~

HOME ON THE RANGE

With the cook, the new butler named Grange
Indulged in his antics so strange,
 For he screwed her, the fink,
 In the fridge and the sink,
But she felt he had not found the range.

~~~~~~~

If a girl will not give in an inch,
And from moral behavior won't flinch,
 And she finds it too crass
 To be fucked up the ass,
Then her armpit will do in a pinch.

~~~~~~~

THE JOCULAR PHILOSOPHER

A noted philosopher, jocular,
Was stopped by a harlot monocular.
    He rejected her ass
    As vulgar and crass
Till she offered him intercourse ocular.

～～～

This one-eyed old harlot named Kim,
The philosopher screwed with such vim,
    That he said, "I'll be back
    When I get some more jack."
So she kept an eye out just for him.

～～～

The learned young linguist Lautrec
Made love to a girl from Quebec,
    And he kissed her, they say,
    À la manière français,
And he finished her off à la Grècque.

～～～

An agile young lady was Lynn;
For money she married old Flynn,
    But his pecker was dead
    So the young lady said,
"When I stand on my head, drop it in."

～～～

WOMEN'S LIB

When the railroad advanced Miss McCord
A new honor for women was scored.
    She was made a conductor,
    But so many men fucked her
She no longer will shout *All Aboard!*

～～～

ALL IN THE FAMILY

There was a young man named McGraw
Who had an affair with his ma.
 She said, "Give me another,
 You are better than brother."
He said, "No, I must save one for pa."

～～～

There was an embalmer named Moffin
Whose work kept him late very often,
 For when anyone died
 He took personal pride
In laying each corpse in its coffin.

～～～

When John saw his girl, Miss O'Dare,
Remove her fake ass, tits and hair,
 He went into a shock
 As he pulled out his cock
And he fucked all the stuff in the chair.

～～～

The lumberman's daughter, they say,
Appeared somewhat splintered away,
 For her motto, she said,
 When she climbed into bed,
Was to let the chips fall where they may.

～～～

HONOR AT STAKE

An old two-bit whore name of Shorter
Was engaged by an elderly porter.
 She was so much impressed
 By his vigor and zest
No one asked for or gave any quarter.

～～～

A *FRIEND* INDEED!

The snatch of a girl of South Bend
Was deep and appeared without end.
    She could not get her fill
    Till a plumber named Bill
Plumbed her depths with the help of his *friend*.

~~~~~~

A simple young girl was beguiled
By suitors who every night dialed,
    And they smiled with delight
    When they kissed her good-night,
But the lips that they kissed never smiled.

~~~~~~

When Max looked at Anne on the tractor
He pulled out his prick to distract her.
    She encouraged young Max
    So he pulled off his slacks,
And on top of the tractor Max Factor.

~~~~~~

IN THE ALLEY

There was a young fellow named Yost
Who said that his girl was the most.
    She was sick and half-blind,
    In a wheelchair confined,
But was super when hung on a post.

~~~~~~

The harlot that's smarter avoids
Disaster of work stoppage voids
    From a pregnancy lapse
    Or a case of the claps
By insuring her pussy with Lloyds.

~~~~~~

A lady of joy and adventure
Was fucked by a pervert named Bencher.
     When he left, she had gas
     And a pain in the ass,
Till the doctor removed Bencher's denture.

~~~~~

MERIT BADGE
The busy street frightened Miss Blue,
Till Boy Scouts assisted her through.
     She asked, "Can I repay
     Your good deed for today?"
Said the leader, "A blow job will do."

~~~~~

A worldly old lady named Blugg
Was floored by an anxious young thug.
     She said to him, "Sire,
     You had better try higher
For I fear you are licking the rug."

~~~~~

NO APPLES IN EDEN
In the Garden of Eden man's fate
Was settled when Eve took the bait,
     But it wasn't an apple
     With which Eve had to grapple,
It was Adam's banana she ate.

~~~~~

There was an old harlot named Blake
Whose price made a young sailor quake.
     He had thought to complain,
     But he found in the main
That she gave all the lads a fair shake.

~~~~~

PLAY BALL!

The players were irked by Miss Thatcher;
In yelling no ball fan could match her.
    She was fucked on the mound
    By the pitcher renowned,
And again on home plate by the catcher.

~~~~~

I THOUGHT YOU'D NEVER ASK

To the doctor went old Mr. Frick,
And the nurse said, "Lie down, you look sick.
    "Tell me, what can I do
    Till the doc can see you?"
So he asked her to suck on his prick.

~~~~~

The fear, said a nurse named Miss Glock,
Of drowning would send her in shock.
    It was known to all folk
    She could not swim a stroke,
But was often found down on the doc.

~~~~~

SAVE FACE

To her boyfriend, a lady named Grace
Said her cunthole had rags set in place.
    Said her boyfriend, so grave,
    "Though your cunt we can't save,
You can still find a way to save face."

~~~~~

STRANGE TAIL

There was a young fairy named Gray
Who dated a Lesbian one day.
    They agreed that they knew
    Who'd do what, how, to who,
But they could not agree who should pay.

~~~~~

A madam of no mean ability
Developed a fine new facility
    For outcasts discarded
    And the mental retarded
And those in the prime of senility.

~~~~~

HOLY DAY

There was a young lady named Grunday
Who fucked every day except Sunday,
    When she rested her box
    By sucking on cocks,
For the Lord's Day must not be a fun day.

~~~~~

MAN'S BEST FRIEND

When Johnny was dating Miss Jean,
He complained of her cunt which was green
    And all covered with mold,
    But he soon was consoled—
She got Fido to lick it off clean.

~~~~~

NOT HUNGRY

Coming home late at night, Mr. Keaton
Did appear to his wife somewhat beaten.
    She lay down on the bed
    And her pussy she spread,
But he said he had already eaten.

~~~~~

There was a young Scotsman named Keith
Who said to his girl on the heath,
    "What I'd like, Miss MacLouth,
    Is a bust in the mouth."
But she gave him a crack in the teeth.

~~~~~

A girl of great height was Miss Hunt;
Her man was a very small runt.
     When in front he did face her
     And reached up to embrace her,
He was faced with a faceful of cunt.

~~~~~

"The man that I want," said Miss Kell,
"Will buy dinner and drinks for a spell,
     And with little persuasion
     He will snatch on occasion
A sweet kiss and vice versa as well."

~~~~~

THAT'S THE WAY IT IS IN SWEDEN

Though the butler proceeded to lick,
He failed to erect the King's prick.
     Said the butler, "Your Majesty—
     Indeed, what a travesty!
How come that my ass does the trick?"

~~~~~

The English professor, MacMeech,
Was fondling a girl on the beach.
     She said, "Shall we fuck?"
     But he said to her, "Suck—
For *fuck* is a figure of speech."

~~~~~

To the lab went the cunt of Miss Phipps;
From whoring she cashed in her chips.
     It was pilfered en route
     By a mailman hirsute,
Who got chancres and sores on the lips.

~~~~~

A man and his wife name of Pickett
Had boarded the train with no ticket.
    This made the conductor
    So mad that he fucked her,
And when through he forced Pickett to lick it.

<hr>

A lady of learning named Roma
Learned much while at school in Tacoma.
    Her instructor had sucked her
    And her principal fucked her
For a *Summa Cum Laude* diploma.

<hr>

A stork is a bird, so they say,
Which brings in nine months and a day
    A bundle of joy,
    An infant so coy—
But a swallow keeps babies away.

<hr>

Down the street walking backward went Sears
With his cock hanging out, it appears.
    Said a lady in shock,
    "You're exposing your cock!"
But he said he was trolling for queers.

<hr>

SEPARATE THE MEN FROM THE BOYS

The Grecians are famed for fine art
And buildings and stone work so smart.
    They distinguish with poise
    The young men from the boys,
And use crowbars to keep them apart.

<hr>

On a date with a lad went Miss Flo;
She was asked for a fuck, but said, "No,
    You can go second class,
    Shove your prick up my ass—
I am saving my cunt for my beau."

A thoughtful old fellow named Keaton
Observed that his whore was moth-eaten,
    But this man was sagacious
    And he found it more gracious
To depart from the path that was beaten.

A sordid old whore from Lapeer
Was fucked in the ass from the rear,
    And her pussy smelled sweeter
    For there issued a peter
Which had lodged in her crotch for a year.

To his dad said a lad name of Neals,
"I'm aware how a piece of ass feels,
    For I've had my first screw,
    And I'll have some more, too,
Just as soon as my orifice heals."

SHORT-TERM DEPOSIT

A banker, hardpressed, name of Paul,
The handwriting saw on the wall.
    He was broke and demented,
    So his asshole he rented,
With a charge for an early withdrawal.

TRUE FRIEND

A companion, sincere and refined,
Is the Persian, the best you will find.
    To the bittermost end
    He remains a staunch friend
Who will not leave his buddy's behind.

~~~~~~

There was a young lady named Tweek
Whose pussy was flabby and weak,
    But her asshole was tight
    So she cried with delight,
"I'm so glad that I married a Greek!"

~~~~~~

There was a young maid unaware,
Who married a sheepherder fair,
    And he said, somewhat gruff,
    "You must learn how to stuff
Both your feet in the hip boots I wear."

~~~~~~

The whore to the Pope did appeal,
"Save my soul—before Christ I will kneel."
    Said the Pope to the whore,
    "You may go—sin no more.
But be sure when you fuck it's for real."

~~~~~~

A horny old bishop named Bart
Made buggery a very fine art.
    He performed so superior
    At the papal posterior
That the Pope had no time for a fart.

~~~~~~

The fearless old Bishop of Brest
Put his faith in the Lord to the test.
In the apse he fucked whores
Who had chancres and sores,
But first they were sprinkled and blessed.

~~~~~~~

THE BEST PART

As Graham for God madly dashes,
His mind is disturbed by strange flashes.
He believes, when he dies,
Like the Phoenix he'll rise,
But his asshole will rise from the ashes.

~~~~~~~

There was an old bishop named Dunn
Who screwed an old lady for fun.
Then he wrote her a letter—
Said her daughter was better
And her mother was second to nun.

~~~~~~~

The monk at the calendar glances,
Then he picks out a nun and he prances
With his head bowed in prayer
To a niche in his lair
And in his retreat makes advances.

~~~~~~~

"Poor drunk," said a Salvation chick,
"Your choice for the faith must be quick.
'Twas for you Jesus died."
But the drunkard replied,
"I did not even know he was sick."

~~~~~~~

In the crypt an old priest named Ignatius
Was fucking a Sister flirtatious.
    He said, "I have often
    Fucked nuns on a coffin,
But never has one been so spacious."

~~~~~~

As he spread an old nun, Father Keating
Checked her heart to be sure it was beating,
    Then his head he did bare
    And he said a short prayer,
For he always said *Grace* before eating.

~~~~~~

Miss Master said no man outclassed her;
The pastor, past master, surpassed her.
    When the pastor had passed her
    His disaster came faster,
The past master became the passed pastor.

~~~~~~

A horny old bishop named Schleft
Plunged his prick in a worn-out nun's cleft,
    But her cunt was so spacious
    That he said, "Goodness gracious!
For a moment I thought you had left."

~~~~~~

BARGAIN HUNTER

At confession a fellow named Spence
Described his cock-sucking offence.
    Said the priest, "For your wrong
    You must suck on my dong,
But I only will pay fifty cents."

~~~~~~

To the Pope, said the Bishop of Strand,
"I've a birth control method so grand.
    The solution, I fear,
    May not be very clear,
But I have it right here in my hand."

~~~~~~

The priest makes an offer vicarial:
Good life in the afterworld aerial.
    And his motto: Don't Sin.
    He gets fat—you get thin.
You will get for your pains, decent burial.

~~~~~~

At the church the new preacher of Wheeling
Gave the girls an oration with feeling.
    When he showed them his dong
    Over ten inches long,
All the belles in the church started peeling.

~~~~~~

DOG DAYS

There was a young girl of Calais
Who had seven dogs to display.
    All their names were unique—
    After days of the week,
And she said every dog had his day.

~~~~~~

A stalwart young fellow named Galion
Was given the Pervert's Medallion,
    For he buggered a cow
    As he stood on a sow,
While he sucked off a Percheron stallion.

~~~~~~

In bed climbed the dog of Miss Grogg;
This put her young man in a fog.
    When he said to her, "Darling,
    Tell me, why are you snarling?"
She said, "Why are you fucking the dog?"

~~~~~~~

While out on the farm, Mr. Jay
Saw a lad fucking pigs in the hay.
    Said Jay, "Why you brat!
    Tell me who taught you that?
Stand back and I'll show you the way."

~~~~~~~

UNTIL DEATH DO YOU PART
The sheepherder came with his knife
To slaughter a sheep for his wife.
    Said the sheep, "Why you freak,
    It was only last week
That you promised to love me for life."

~~~~~~~

"This plot," said old farmer McGraw,
"I hold in great reverence and awe,
    For my first piece of ass
    I had here on the grass,
While her mother stood near and said 'Baa.' "

~~~~~~~

To the madam said old man McNish,
"A fuck that is novel I wish.
    I've fucked sheep, goat and gnu,
    And a jackrabbit too.
Tell me, what do you have in a fish?"

~~~~~~~

Said a girl who was laid 'neath the pines,
"You give a great fuck, Mr. Hines."
    He said, "At the zoo
    I learned how to screw
By throwing the meat to the lions."

～～～～

The miner, it seems, undertook
To fucking his mule by the brook.
    He said, "Bless my hide;
    I'd make her my bride,
If only she knew how to cook."

～～～～

At the wedding, so nervous was Bart
That he pissed in his pants at the start.
    When the priest spoke his bit,
    He proceeded to shit,
And the nuptials were sealed with a fart.

～～～～

The sparrow and horse have begun
A friendship that's second to none.
    This is proof, I submit,
    That if one can eat shit,
Then two can live cheaply as one.

～～～～

At a contest for farting in Butte
A lady's mutation was cute.
    It won a diploma
    For fetid aroma
When three judges were felled by the brute.

～～～～

A flatulent whore name of Mame
Broke wind without feelings of shame.
     Her farts were so rotten
     They were never forgotten,
For she honored each fart with a name.

~~~~~~

An intrepid old man of Azores
Engaged one of the dirtiest whores.
     In her twat was a blight
     Which he licked with delight,
And he fucked all her festering sores.

~~~~~~

When Jane viewed the prod of young Bert,
She cried, "Oh my God, will it hurt?"
     But Bert lit a match
     And ignited her snatch
And went down for the flaming dessert.

~~~~~~

Ten men who were shipwrecked connived
To find food until searchers arrived.
     Nine had morals and pride
     And these poor fellows died,
But the cocksucker, Pierre, he survived.

~~~~~~

For busy young typist, Miss Fry,
Advancement no boss could deny.
     To the top she did climb
     Just by coming on time
And by eating her lunch on the fly.

~~~~~~

The butcher's apprentice, Miss Gossage,
Observed on her cunt a green moss edge.
    Said the doctor, "How quaint,
    From a man's meat it ain't,
And it tastes just like smoked liver sausage."

~~~~~

When making banana cake, Joel
Put fruit and two eggs in the hole
    'Tween two legs and proceeded
    To cream nicely as needed,
And he finished by licking the bowl.

~~~~~

To the druggist, a man of Lapeer
Said, "You've cunts made of rubber, I hear."
    Said the druggist, "We do.
    Shall I wrap one for you?"
He said, "No, I will eat it right here."

~~~~~

Some men have a taste hard to match;
The feeblest excuses they'll hatch.
    They will raise a big stink
    For a hair in their drink,
But think nothing of eating a snatch.

~~~~~

While dining, a fellow named Nick
In his stew found an elephant's prick.
    Said the waiter, "Don't hunt,
    Someone just found a cunt;
If you're nice he might give you a lick."

~~~~~

A moral young lady named Pease
Stuffed her pussy with lunch meat and cheese.
A man took her to bed
And he ate it with bread
And he said, "Pass the beer, if you please."

~~~~~~

TOCCATA FOR ORGAN
When Bach strayed too far, he repented,
For hunger pangs gnawed and tormented.
By luck passed a maid
And her crotch she displayed
And thus was the Bach's lunch invented.

~~~~~~

When purchasing cheese, Mr. Scott
Would examine with care the whole lot.
He would make a selection
When he got an erection
From the cheeses which smelled like a twat.

~~~~~~

A young man raped a lady named Cole
And it tickled her heart and her soul,
So she ran home and said
To her dear husband Fred,
"All these years we have used the wrong hole!"

~~~~~~

There was an old lady who flipped
And lived all alone in a crypt,
All because flies she hated
With a hate unbated,
Until one day a fly she unzipped.

~~~~~~

The noted psychologist Gluck
Observed that some ladies were stuck
In the depths of depression,
So with learned discretion
He taught the old bitches to fuck.

~~~~~

THE UNSEAMLY SEAMSTRESS
In a bind was a seamstress of Hasting—
She spent her time sewing and basting.
It was needles to say
She did not mend her way,
Sew it seams that her hole life was wasting.

~~~~~

In Lachine lived an old maid named Jean;
She was raped as she passed a ravine.
She was left much deranged
For her will was arranged
To construct more ravines in Lachine.

~~~~~

There was an old lady of Lissing
Who discovered what she had been missing.
She was fucked on the sod
And she cried: "Oh, my God!
All these years it was just used for pissing!"

~~~~~

There was an old maid name of Minnie
Who chanced to observe a lad skinny
As he beat on his meat,
So she said, "Come in, sweet;
That is love's labor lost, you dumb ninny."

~~~~~

PERHAPS IN A HAYSTACK

The doctor examined Miss Pask;
He took the old spinster to task.
    He said, "What I'm thinking
    You will have to stop drinking,
For you'll not find a prick in a flask."

~~~~~~~

The panties of old spinster Tweek
Dropped down in a mishap unique
    At a twat exhibition—
    It was judged mint condition
And it won the first prize for antique.

~~~~~~~

KNIGHT LIFE

The bulge up in front was apparent
Which made the young maid incoherent.
    She explained a bad day
    Was the cause of dismay,
But the truth was a knight had been errant.

~~~~~~~

To the doc went a maid in dejection;
He examined her twat with reflection.
    "What you need is a screw
    For that pussy brand new.
I'll prescribe you some love and erection."

~~~~~~~

ASP IN THE ALFALFA

In Hawaii a lady named Cass
Had a belly that swelled up a mass.
    At a dance, she did blurt,
    When she wore a grass skirt
She encountered a snake in the grass.

~~~~~~~

A lady proceeded to curse
Her child with his antics perverse.
"He's brought nothing but shame
And he's sullied my name,
And the fuck that he came from was worse."

~~~~~

A girl thought it wise to divulge
The reason her belly did bulge:
"It is not pie and cheese
Which expands my chemise,
I suspect it's the sport I indulge."

~~~~~

THE BUTLER DONE IT!

When Mary's new baby was due
She confessed to her mother she knew
That the chef was to blame,
And her mother said, "Shame,
I'm afraid that he's your father too."

~~~~~

A wretched old whore of Algiers
Was judged in the court by her peers,
But the jury dismissed her
For the foreman had kissed her,
And the judge was a month in arrears.

~~~~~

A whore who much trade did attract
Fell dead in the midst of a pact.
Twenty men with no hitch
Paid for screwing the bitch
Before anyone noticed the fact.

~~~~~

FIVE MORE MINUTES

While fucking a whore, Mr. Binks
Observed that she died from some kinks
    Which her cunt did invade.
    But said Binks, "Since I've paid,
I will fuck the old bitch till she stinks."

〜〜〜〜

A lady of joy, young and bold,
Offered ass to a man for some gold.
    The man was beguiled
    By her warmth as she smiled,
But the ass that she sold was ice-cold.

〜〜〜〜

A whore on the railroad, Miss Burrage,
The overtime screw would discourage.
    A conductor named Tiding
    Fucked too long on the siding,
So she charged the old fellow demurrage.

〜〜〜〜

BETTER THAN SNIFFING GLUE

A man short of cash name of Cliff
Told a whore that her price was too stiff,
    And he asked how much fuck
    He could get for a buck,
So she told him she'd give him a sniff.

〜〜〜〜

The liquor of naive young Cotter
Was soaked up by whores like a blotter.
    They drank only straight drinks,
    So said Cotter, "Methinks
You can lead whores to drink, but not water."

〜〜〜〜

"We're here," said two harlots of Daucus,
"To tour through the White House so raucous,
　　For we have an obsession
　　To see Congress in session,
And to see if the Senate will caucus."

〜〜〜

At the brothel, a man from Djibouti
Took his pick of the harlots, a cutie.
　　But the madam said, "Nay,
　　For the union rules say
You will have to take age before beauty."

〜〜〜

A horny old man of Dubuque
Made a deal with a harlot, a fluke,
　　But her cunt was so foul
　　That he said, with a scowl,
"Tell me, where is your pisspot to puke?"

〜〜〜

To a whore a young fellow named Elliot
Said, "Dear, can I stay on your belly yet?"
　　She said, "Sir, you have gall.
　　I've ten drunks in the hall,
And I still have to fuck Father Kelly yet."

〜〜〜

There was an old man somewhat foggy
Who fucked an old harlot so scroggy
　　That he asked the old hag
　　To put some in a bag
And he took a piece home to his doggy.

〜〜〜

The old miner inserted a funnel
In the cunt of a whore named Miss Bunnel.
    Then he shouted with glee
    And he said, "I can see
There's a light at the end of the tunnel!"

<hr />

It appears the Machine Age was gaining
On the whores of a madam named Blaining.
    The machines could fuck faster
    And new tricks they did master,
So the whores were sent out for retraining.

<hr />

A haggard old bitch name of Gleek
Was forty-five years past her peak,
    But her profits did soar
    And she made more and more
For the thing that she sold was antique.

<hr />

At the doctor's, a whore name of Glover
When checked for her health did discover
    A run-down condition,
    So said her physician,
"You must stay out of bed to recover."

<hr />

A battered old harlot named Greer
Decided to quit her career.
    From a fuck she arose
    With her hand at her nose.
"I have had it," she said, "up to here."

<hr />

ELECTRONIC AGE

Said a man to the madam, Miss Grout:
"Do you have any free whores about?"
    The old madam serene
    Checked her monitor screen—
"There's a trucker," she said, "pulling out."

~~~~~

The whore that was picked up by Hearst
Looked so badly worn that he cursed,
    So he asked her how long
    She'd been taking the dong.
"I've just started," she said, "you're the first."

~~~~~

STRATOCRUISER

In flight a young hostess named Jane
Improved on her pay with no strain,
    But she peddled no meat
    Below ten thousand feet,
For she worked on a much higher plane.

~~~~~

A misinformed lady was Gertie;
She had her first fuck at age thirty.
    So she said, "It is clear
    That my mother was queer,
For she told me that fucking was dirty."

~~~~~

In the church an old trollop named Kay
Knelt her down in a reverent way.
    Said the preacher with gravity,
    "You are saved from depravity."
But she said, "It's for piece that I pray."

~~~~~

SMART-ASS LAWYERS

There was a young coed of Kent,
In matters of law eloquent.
    She told lawyers from Yale
    That her ass was for sale,
But they proved it was only for rent.

~~~~~~

A sordid old whore from Lahore
Would fuck till her asshole was sore,
    And her cunt was more hairy
    Than the sweet Virgin Mary,
And she never got pregnant, what's more.

~~~~~~

NO CARRYING CHARGES

Let's give credit to old harlot Klutz
For the way she sold ass—it took guts.
    With her added refinement
    You could fuck on consignment,
And could pay after blowing your nuts.

~~~~~~

A pregnant young lady named Kant
Was asked who had been her gallant.
    "When it's wild oats you sow
    Tell me how can you know
Which seed grew which singular plant?"

~~~~~~

A peglegged lady named Lunt
Could always sell plenty of cunt.
    It was not by deceit
    That she peddled her meat,
But by putting her best leg out front.

~~~~~~

INFLATION

To the call-girl went horny young Mahler,
But her price made the poor fellow holler,
So he said, "I would pay
The high buck for a lay
If your pussy would shrink like the dollar."

~~~~~~

EMISSION PROBLEM

An old harlot inept named McLure,
Sold five thousand fucks that were poor.
But complaints did her in
And she paid for her sin,
Since a recall she had to endure.

~~~~~~

MIND YOUR P'S AND Q'S

A studious harlot was Metters
Who always was screwed by her betters.
She'd collect B.V.D.'s
From well-known Ph.D.'s;
She was truly a lady of letters.

~~~~~~

A pregnant young lady named Nettie
Could blame either John, Joe or Freddie,
Or it could have been Thackeray,
Or from Aaron to Zachary,
For her mother said, "You can't go steady."

~~~~~~

Said a whore to a fellow named Meyer,
"It is fifty for fucking me, sire."
"I'll save money," he swore,
So he married the whore,
But he found that the price was now higher.

~~~~~~

TRAVEL FIRST CLASS

In Scotland far out on the moor,
As shown in Cook's travel brochure,
    Lives a harlot named Fitch
    With her niche for the rich
And her asshole for those that are poor.

FAIRNESS DOCTRINE

A state-controlled brothel in Natchez
Was ruled by Fair Practice dispatches.
    You would get, by priorities,
    Worn out whores from minorities,
Or old harlots with handicapped snatches.

The State meat inspector named Pete
Worked evenings for madam LaFitte,
    Where he checked every twat
    For decay or for rot,
And he passed on each customer's meat.

A half-wit young fellow named Newt
Was thought by relations as cute.
    He went over to auntie's
    And got into her panties
And this harmless relation bore fruit.

In the cunt of a dead whore named Phipp
Was installed a new silicon chip,
    So the feedback from sensors
    Went to coils and condensers,
And she fucked with new vigor and zip.

IS THERE A CHOICE?

To a whore a young fellow named Pitt
Complained that her crotch was not fit,
    For her cunt had no wool;
    Said the whore, affable,
"Did you come here to fuck or to knit?"

～～～～

Said the priest, on our knees we must pray
For the cunts of old whores that decay.
    At one time it was free,
    Then they charged a large fee,
And they now cannot give it away.

～～～～

Of the madam, a fellow named Prentiss
Requested one non compos mentis.
    "They're all busy," she said,
    "Sucking cocks that are dead.
Would you care to select an apprentice?"

～～～～

AU CANADA

A hardy old whore of Quebec
At the end of the day was a wreck
    From the moans and the trials
    Of old farts with the piles
And from bastards that breathed down her neck.

～～～～

There was an old whore of St. Paul
Who gave lessons to lads in the hall.
    Her motto was plain,
    There was much they could gain,
For before one can walk one must crawl.

～～～～

COLD CUTS FOR COLD CUTS

A lady of joy on the street
Was stopped by a butcher discreet,
    For this man was beguiled
    By her warmth as she smiled,
But she sold him a cold cut of meat.

~~~~~~~

A harlot, picked up on the street,
Was charged with dispensing her meat.
    She remarked in defense
    That she meant no offence,
And she offered the jury a treat.

~~~~~~~

When John licked a harlot named Susie,
He slobbered all over the floozie,
    So she said to him, "John,
    Let's go out on the lawn,
And I'll show you how dogs lick my coozie."

~~~~~~~

A low-priced old harlot of Thrace
Enticed a young man to her place,
    But he said to her, "Nellie,
    You must lay on your belly,
For I can't stand to look at your face."

~~~~~~~

AT THE NURSING HOME

A soft-hearted whore named Miss Tuckem
Would take on poor cripples and fuck 'em,
    And those lame, halt and blind,
    And in wheelchairs confined—
If they needed a blow-job, she'd suck 'em.

~~~~~~~

An elderly harlot of Twitting
Received an award upon quitting—
    Well-preserved in a crock
    Was an elephant's cock—
And she said the award was most fitting.

~~~~~

A sordid old harlot named Weiss
A bearded old man did entice.
    Between panting and wheezes
    He maintained he was Jesus,
So she let the old bastard come twice.

~~~~~

Complained an old harlot named Wertz:
"My business of late badly hurts.
    At times it is slow—
    Men come and they go—
And sometimes they come in big spurts."

~~~~~

METROPOLITAN OPERA STAR
When her fistula drained in her ano
She would scream from the pain and guano.
    Said old Bing, "Do not fret,
    You can sing at the Met
As a coloratura soprano."

~~~~~

There was an old whore of Belgrade
Whose chancres had left her dismayed.
    She sought help from Doc Gray
    But had no cash to pay,
So she offered her service in trade.

~~~~~

THE 4-D'S

If bargains are what you are buying,
A madam all kinds is supplying,
    She has some with Disease,
    And some Dead, if you please,
And some wretches Disabled or Dying.

~~~~~

Since his girl had the clap, Mr. Fritz
Decided the rear hole to blitz,
    Thus avoiding the pox
    Which infested her box,
But his pecker has now got the shits.

~~~~~

A lonely old maid name of Kate
Had trouble in finding a date.
    An old man who was stiff
    Took a sniff of her quiff
And said, "Kate, I'm afraid it's too late!"

~~~~~

There was an old whore named McFink
Whose pussy was rotten, I think.
    She was fucked for an hour
    By old Cardinal Bower,
For that's all he could take of the stink.

~~~~~

A philosopher, walking the shore,
Was ignoring the pleas of a whore,
    But he said he would screw
    If she had something new,
So she offered a festering sore.

~~~~~

A simple young lady alluring
Thought the ditch-digger's cock was enduring,
But the rigger's was bigger,
And he fucked with such vigor
That her asshole was torn from its mooring.

~~~~~~

A widow who lived in Berlin
Cut the cock off her dead husband Flynn.
Up his dead ass she shoved it
And she said, "He'd have loved it!
It's the only hole it's not been in."

~~~~~~

A surgeon who hailed from Cape Horn
Had rebuilt a cock that was worn,
But his climaxing feat
Was replacing the meat
On a snatch that was tattered and torn.

~~~~~~

Said the doctor with fingers so deft,
As he probed in an old lady's cleft,
"From the wear, I would say,
It's eroding away,
And you only have fourteen fucks left."

~~~~~~

A MATTER OF SEMANTICS
In Japan a young Yank with elation
Asked a whore for a new sex creation.
But he went into shock
When she bit off his cock,
For the meaning was lost in translation.

~~~~~~

From a madam, a fellow named Gore
Selected her lowest priced whore.
    When he gave her a goose
    Her right titty came loose
And her pussy dropped down to the floor.

~~~~~

A discomposed lady of Guelph
Would daily assemble herself
    With her wig, a glass eye,
    Her peg leg all awry,
And her cunt which she kept on the shelf.

~~~~~

There was an old scientist, Hill,
Who swallowed a nuclear pill.
    The reaction corroded
    His balls, which exploded,
And his asshole was found in Brazil.

~~~~~

An ingenious old chemist named Hugh
Brought some hope to the faltering screw.
    He concocted one day
    A new vaginal spray
Which made worn-out old cunts smell like new.

~~~~~

A careless young fellow named Kline
Was fucking a whore serpentine.
    In the midst of her throes
    She bit off his nose.
He thanked God it was not sixty-nine.

~~~~~

When her dear husband died, Mrs. Newt
Was sad, 'cause she missed the old coot,
    So she cut off his balls,
    Which she hung on the walls,
And his prick she made into a flute.

~~~~~~~

A thalidomide baby was Pete;
He was born with his arms incomplete,
    But he did not lament
    This most tragic event,
He could still beat his meat with his feet.

~~~~~~~

There was an old widow who raised
The sheet on her dead man and praised
    What she sucked on for years,
    Then she cropped it with shears,
For she wanted to sample it braised.

~~~~~~~

While hunting, some buckshot hit Springer
And some of it passed through his dinger.
    When he pissed, spray would shoot
    Through the holes like a flute,
Till a flutist taught Springer to finger.

~~~~~~~

A broken-down harlot did tremble
When violently fucked by young Kemble.
    He said, "Let's have another."
    But she said, "Hold it, brother,
For my cunt I must now reassemble."

~~~~~~~

A battered old whore with a worn hole
Was put on the street with her torn hole,
  But her ass was not worn
  So she sold it for corn,
And it got to be known as the corn hole.

≈≈≈≈

Miss Fern did attach to the churn
A dildoe, and started to turn
  The cream into butter
  With nary a flutter;
When the butter was made, so was Fern.

≈≈≈≈

SELF-SERVICE
A man with himself made alliance—
Shoved his cock up his ass in defiance,
  And he mocked every moral
  Whether written or oral,
And defied every law known to science.

≈≈≈≈

DOUBLE JEOPARDY
There was a streetwalker discreet
Who would not cut her price for a treat,
  For she said prices low
  Would not bring enough dough,
And she'd find herself out on the street.

≈≈≈≈

HAIR RESTORER
A distracted young mother named Frommes
Spent her time in the church singing psalms,
  For her son, keen and bright,
  Suffered loss in his sight,
And had hair growing thick on his palms.

≈≈≈≈

INDIAN ROPE TRICK

A man from the Cape of Good Hope
With women no longer could cope,
    So to India he went
    With his tool badly bent,
Where he studied the trick with the rope.

〜〜〜

To her date said a lady named Hewitt,
"My mother said I mustn't do it.
    She advised against fucking
    But said nothing of sucking—
Would you mind if I licked it and blew it?"

〜〜〜

THE SNERD

A bicycle buff name of Keats
Watched the girls doing bicycle feats,
    And right after they raced
    He ran over in haste
To sniff at the bicycle seats.

〜〜〜

A feeble old fellow named Kregg
Was fucking a whore with one leg.
    He could not make the grade
    And the whore was dismayed,
So she finished herself with her peg.

〜〜〜

A rugged old lumberman Lee
Wed a one-legged maid of Dundee,
    For he saw by the grain
    That her peg did contain
The knothole he fucked in a tree.

〜〜〜

At Christmas a lady named Plum
Presented her bare-naked bum
    And asked Santa to fuck,
    But old Santa said, "Yuck,
Down the chimney I've already come."

~~~~~~

Said the daughter to mother, "Some slick
Put his hand in my panties real quick
    And he fondled my twat,
    But I fixed the young snot
When I fondled the knob of his dick."

~~~~~~

In the dark a young fellow named River
A fuck to his wife did deliver,
    But after he came,
    He said, "It's the same
As fucking a pound of warm liver."

~~~~~~

LEARN THE ROPES

The puppeteer's helper, Miss Tuppet,
Was madly in love with a puppet,
    So she said, "Puppeteer,
    Can you pull some strings dear,
And instruct my young puppet to up it?"

~~~~~~

"My poor back," said a man, "I did twist it,
And my sex life—for years I have missed it."
    The doc's nurse, young in years,
    Heard his story in tears,
So she stood on her head and he kissed it.

~~~~~~

67

The brown-noser, Joe, did amass
A great many points, but alas,
    When his boss died of flu
    They interred poor Joe too,
For Joe's nose was stuck firm in his ass.

~~~~~~~

While checking her cash, madam Fern
Found counterfeit bills from young Bern.
    Though she ran up the stair
    He was already there
At the point where there was no return.

~~~~~~~

THE DISSIDENT
The toy makers started anew
With weapons of war as they do,
    But one man, we must mention,
    Went against the convention
By inventing a doll that would screw..

~~~~~~~

PLAYING HER CARDS
An avid bridge player astute
Observed his opponent so cute
    As she raised up her dress
    To promote a finesse,
But he noted it was not hirsute.

~~~~~~~

FIRST THINGS FIRST
By the side of the road stood Miss Barr;
Her battery was not up to par.
    Said a driver named Gump,
    "Can I give you a jump?"
She said, "Yes, if you first start my car."

~~~~~~~

A noted old chemist named Bayer
Was lauded at lunch by the mayor.
    They all asked to be shown
    How he made the hormone;
He replied, he neglected to pay her.

In Zurich old clockmaker Chase
Improved on the clock commonplace.
    He made one of fine brass
    With two feet and an ass
In the place of two hands and a face.

A song was composed by young Chuck
But the lyrics ran into bad luck.
    Though devoid of all flaws
    It fell short just because
Of the title: *With Love You Don't Fuck.*

With his lot man has not been contented;
By compulsion to change he's tormented.
    At improvement he strains,
    But the screw still remains
Just as good as it first was invented.

The cat in the rocket was curled
And out into space it was hurled.
    Its owner, Miss May,
    In truth now could say
That her pussy was out of this world.

HONORABLE ENTERPRISE

A noted inventor named Dan
Proceeded according to plan
    To construct a device
    At a moderate price
For deflecting the shit from the fan.

A mathematician named Dare
Could issue a turd that was square,
    Then he tried an ejection
    With a rhombus trisection—
I believe that he's still straining there.

A virgin is tender and dear,
But much like a bubble, I fear.
    The virgin and bubble
    Each face the same trouble,
For a prick will make both disappear.

Beneath his piano, young Deever
Discovered his dying retriever.
    Sometime later that day
    He met greater dismay—
'Neath his organ he found a dead beaver.

By wives many men are demented,
Deceived and abused and tormented,
    So I say, men, beware,
    And avoid this despair—
Why own the damn thing, you can rent it.

THE FLAT-CHESTED HARLOT

A whore who had not used discretion
To the doctor explained her depression.
 Her complaints, she did mention,
 Were arising from tension,
But to him it looked more like compression.

~~~~~~~

A squalid old whore name of Funks
Would fuck only junkies and drunks,
 But her daughter prodigious
 Was profoundly religious
And consorted with friars and monks.

~~~~~~~

A lad with his life was disgusted
And he wished that his dad had not lusted,
 But it wasn't the lust,
 For his dad put his trust
In a rubber so worn that it busted.

~~~~~~~

CONDITIONED REFLEX

The White Russian general embarks
To pick up some whores in the parks.
 One exposes her crack
 But the general draws back—
It reminds him too much of Karl Marx.

~~~~~~~

THE SQUARE ROOT OF EWING

A mathematician was Ewing—
His cock was in need of renewing,
 But for years he got by
 With his formula sly,
Which was using a square root for screwing.

~~~~~~~

THE VOICE OF EXPERIENCE

While taking a walk in the fall
Two bulls saw some cows in the kraal.
    Said the young bull, "Let's run
    And we'll each fuck us one."
Said the old bull, "Let's walk and fuck all."

~~~~~~

DON'T HORSE AROUND

Young ladies on bikes can ride far
And their status with men is at par,
    But when ladies ride straddle
    On an old Western saddle
It is stretching a good thing too far.

~~~~~~

TEST TICKLE

Some women are fun, some are fickle;
By some you'll be left in a pickle.
    Put them all to a test,
    Get the one who laughs best,
And the test that is best—a test tickle.

~~~~~~

A whore who turned nun, felt a lack
And sought out her old madam's shack.
    Said the madam, Miss Hood,
    "Have you come back for good?"
She said, "No, it's for evil I'm back."

~~~~~~

DIVORCE

A horny young fellow named Fitch
Engaged an old whore for his itch,
    But he blew on the floor
    As he felt for her bore,
So said, "Give me my cash back, you bitch!"

~~~~~~

NAILED

The queen from attackers once flew
And cried when her horse dropped a shoe,
   "Oh, my kingdom will fail
   For the want of a nail!"
But the kingdom was saved for a screw.

~~~~~~

TAIL OF GLOOM

A gloomy old whore of St. Claire
Was fucked by a man debonair.
   She told sad tales of woe
   Which depressed the man so,
That he plunged in a slough of despair.

~~~~~~

ILL WIND

There was a young lady named Flo
Who said that she wanted to know
   Did bassoonist Herr Klauth
   Make that noise through his mouth?
The conductor cried, "God, I hope so!"

~~~~~~

A noted tree surgeon named Fogg
Developed a tree that could jog,
   But the tree, fully grown,
   Had a mind of its own,
For it ran out and pissed on a dog.

~~~~~~

BOXING FANS

A well-built young girl of Fort Knox
Was rugged and strong as an ox.
   When she wrestled, fans booed
   For her wrestling was crude,
But they all loved to look at her box.

~~~~~~

DOWN ON THE FARM

The pastors berated Miss Fox
For corrupting the men in their flocks.
    Said the winsome young charmer,
    "I'm a mere poultry farmer
Since I spend all my time raising cocks."

～～～～

There was a young fellow named Kissel
Whose asshole was ripped by a missile.
    It was mended with strips
    Which they took from his lips,
And now through his ass he can whistle.

～～～～

CACHE CROP

There was a young lady named Fox
Who planted an acre of cocks.
    They grew up firm and strong.
    Over twelve inches long,
And she stuffed them all into her box.

～～～～

PRICE OF LIBERATION

If a woman must really be free
And with men hold her place equally,
    She must wear up in front
    A man's fly at her cunt,
And must learn how to stand up to pee.

～～～～

BOWLER'S HEADACHE

When he bowled, a young fellow named Fritz
Gave his team a bad case of the fits,
    For he left 10 and 4
    Standing up on the floor.
"I'm accustomed," he said, "to bad splits."

～～～～

While grinding his meat, butcher Girk
Lost his balance because of a quirk.
    He fell into the hopper
    With his ass in the chopper,
And he thus got behind in his work.

~~~~~

To the doctor went old Mrs. Glitz
For she had a bad case of the shits.
    But old Doctor Pitman
    Was strictly a tit man,
And he asked her, "Please show me your tits."

~~~~~

FASHION GIRL
At a contest, a lady named Gog
Took part in a quiz dialogue.
    Asked what fashions she knew,
    She replied she knew two—
One was *Paris*, the other was *dog*.

~~~~~

KEYHOLE SYNDROME
A forgetful professor was Gore;
His actions his wife would abhor.
    He caused nothing but strife
    When he slammed his dear wife
And proceeded to fuck with the door.

~~~~~

At the sperm bank, a lady named Gore
Used her wiles to attract many more.
    When she raised up her dress
    With ingenious finesse,
The depositors came by the score.

~~~~~

The home of a lady named Grace
Did prompt a libidinous race.
    Just the experts could see
    Who the winners would be—
They were fucking all over the place.

Said the priest to a harlot, O'Keefe,
"Your response to the faith is too brief."
    She replied, "By comparison,
    A well-overhung Saracen
Will do more to enhance my belief."

BOTANICAL INTERLUDE

John showed his fine plants to whore Gulcher;
She sneered, "Pour a drink for me, vulture."
    So said John, "I do think
    You can lead whores to drink
But you cannot lead a horticulture."

DISQUALIFIED

A playful young fellow was Gump
Who cherished his ladyfriend's rump.
    "Let's play *Leapfrog*," he said,
    So she lowered her head,
But he never completed the jump.

A young gynecologist, Heep,
Worked long and he often lost sleep,
    For he had an obsession
    To improve his profession,
And his hand in a good thing to keep.

SANCTIFIED SOUP

A moral old fellow named Hicks
From alphabet soup got his kicks.
    He said, "Waiter, make sure
    What you bring me is pure.
Remove all the *SHIT*'s, *CUNT*'s and *PRICK*'s."

~~~~~~

In the cunt of a dead whore named Phipp
Was installed a new silicon chip,
    So the feedback from sensors
    Went to coils and condensers,
And she fucked with new vigor and zip.

~~~~~~

A lady depressed and ill-lucked
By hoodlums was ravaged and fucked.
    Said her lawyer, "Disgrace!
    It's an open, shut case,
But the crime we must now reconstruct."

~~~~~~

SHORTCOMING

An obedient young lady named Hinches
Was not bad at all in the clinches.
    Her ma she'd obey,
    Not to go all the way,
So for years she took only five inches.

~~~~~~

From the train, a young soldier named Jack
Said goodbye, as he leaned out to smack
    The lips of his chick,
    But the train took off quick
And he kissed a cow's ass down the track.

~~~~~~

LEAF AND BULL STORY

A sculptor of note name of Jacques
A beautiful tree carved in rock.
    It was stately and fine
    And a moral design,
For he hid every leaf with a cock.

~~~~~~

Said a man to a harlot, "I wish you
Would wipe off your cunt with this tissue."
    But her pussy still leaked
    And she said, somewhat piqued,
"Please do not make a point of the issue."

~~~~~~

The man who writes *fuck* is a jerk;
He's suspected of having a quirk.
    But the doctor is great
    For he writes *copulate*,
And is paid very well for his work.

~~~~~~

THE STARGAZER

To his wife said astronomer Janus,
"Much renown in the world we will gain us
    When I publish my paper
    On the ungodly vapor
And the rings I have seen on Uranus."

~~~~~~

NEIN!

A near-sighted lady was Kate
Who learned to discern rather late.
    She played with her toys
    With the girls and the boys,
But she knew not her sex until ate.

~~~~~~

THE UNDOING

A fearful young lady named Kippers
Stood in fear of small dogs that were nippers,
    And in fright she would shake
    At the sight of a snake,
But she feared not the snakes behind zippers.

~~~

There was a young girl of Belgrade
With teeth in her snatch where she played.
    An old dentist named Block
    Lost the end of his cock
As he probed for the tooth that decayed.

~~~

When Greeley was fucking Miss Klutz,
She said, as he plunged in his putz,
    "Do you love me, dear Greeley?"
    He answered, "Not really,
I just wanted to blow off my nuts."

~~~

RIGHT HOLE—WRONG PEG

A destitute lady named Laker
Accosted and fucked with a Quaker.
    When she asked him for bread
    He smiled sadly and said,
"If it's bread that you want, fuck a baker."

~~~

OUTHOUSE HONOR

Some names will be famed through the land
And some will be writ in the sand,
    But we'll view names of fools
    While we strain at our stools
Just as long as the shithouse walls stand.

~~~

To Washington went Miss Latrobe,
And by Congress was asked to disrobe.
    By the Congress respected
    She there was subjected
To a thorough Congressional Probe.

~~~~~~

A skilful inventor named Cass
Made a plucker for chickens first class.
    But it seems, and we quote 'im,
    The machine seized his scrotum
And it plucked every hair from his ass.

~~~~~~

THE CHIRPING ZIPPER
To lovers' lane one night went Lear
And he walked in the dark with his dear.
    She said, "Hear all those crickets
    As they chirp in the thickets."
"Those are zippers," he said, "that you hear."

~~~~~~

TEA DRINKER
A simple young fellow named Lee
Flew *TWA* to Dundee.
    When the hostess did say,
    "Coffee *TWA*?"
He said, "No, just *TWAT*."

~~~~~~

DEAD RIGHT!
The old archaeologist, Lew,
Remarked to his wife, "We are through,
    For a mummy I've fucked
    And from this I deduct
That a mummy moves quicker than you."

~~~~~~

BLACK FRIDAY

A redheaded lady named Lize
Sat down and she parted her thighs.
    When a man saw her crack
    He exclaimed, "Why, it's black!"
But the color was due to the flies.

～～～

The professor emeritus Lloyd
New methods of teaching deployed.
    He taught students obscenities
    And other amenities,
So they knew all the words to avoid.

～～～

"I was raped," said the lady of Lyme—
The trial, said the judge, would take time.
    In his chambers he went
    With the lady, and spent
Some time reconstructing the crime.

～～～

CLEAN LIVER

A cautious young fellow named Luntz
Was hailed by a grimy whore once,
    But he said to her, "Gertie,
    Although fucking is dirty,
I fuck only the cleanest of cunts."

～～～

Said the pope to a girl named MacAllister,
"I doubt if you can make my phallus stir."
    But she showed that in Texas
    With her bare solar plexus
She could make every phallus in Dallas stir.

～～～

SINCERE LIP SERVICE?

To the doctor complained old MacMaddit,
"When my prick gets too hard, I have had it.
    This erection's a curse."
    Said the doc's helpful nurse,
"Would you mind if I took a crack at it?"

~~~~~~

Said a man to his girl, Miss MacNurd,
"What's the good word today, have you heard?"
    "The good word for today
    Will be *legs*," she did say,
"And it's time that you spread the good word."

~~~~~~

When Hays hired the typist, Miss May,
He found to his utter dismay
    She could not type a bit
    And was not worth a shit,
So he stroked on her pussy all day.

~~~~~~

PETER PRINCIPLE

While looking for fossils six meters
From basilican altars, Prof. Jeeters
    Claimed to find relics quaint—
    Holy bones of a saint—
But the bones that he found were all peters.

~~~~~~

There was a young bowler named Motch
Whose grip was amazing to watch,
    But the girls were dismayed
    At the time he displayed
His bowling ball grip on their crotch.

~~~~~~

A man screwed his wife and her mother,
Her sisters, her aunts and grandmother.
    On his prick he put glasses
    And he said, "Look for asses,
To be sure we have missed nothing, brother."

~~~~~~

A pedantic old teacher, Miss Brown,
Brought class to the young lads in town.
    She taught Pierre to aspire
    To seek things that were higher,
But Pierre, he did fail and went down.

~~~~~~

TONGUE-TIED KEEPER

There was a zoo keeper named Nick—
A nasty disease made him sick.
    Though there was a time where
    He could lick any bear,
He no longer a pussy could lick.

~~~~~~

To the vet went a fellow named Nixon—
His dog and his cat needed fixin'.
    He said, "Fix the wife, too,
    For she has a loose screw,
And her cunt has had too many pricks in."

~~~~~~

URGE TO PROPAGATE

There was an old botanist, Pace,
Who grew cunts in a pot at his place.
    When they ripened, he'd pluck 'em,
    And he'd eat them or fuck 'em—
They were simpler to grow than to chase.

~~~~~~

POTLICKER

For men that are not up to par,
Be bold, and in life you will star.
  There's no need to get flustered
  If you can't cut the mustard,
You'll do fine if you just lick the jar.

~~~~~

The old hamburg-maker named Pete
Came home every day somewhat beat.
  His wife itched for a lay,
  But he said, "Not today—
All day I've been plunging the meat."

~~~~~

WORLD WAR II VICTIM

A whore who survived Occupation
Was freed by U.S. Liberation,
  But she wore out her ass
  With the army top brass
So she sued and received reparation.

~~~~~

The alphabet soup made by Pease
Was flavored with spices and cheese.
  It was served with liturgy
  To old men of the clergy,
But he took out the C U N T's.

~~~~~

CANIS NOBILIS

A breeder of dogs, somewhat plastered,
A chastity belt for dogs mastered,
  A device to ensure
  That the breeds would be pure,
And no son of a bitch was a bastard.

~~~~~

THE TRANSPLANTS

For a lady, a surgeon named Polk
Switched her cunt and her mouth as a joke.
    It was not all amiss—
    She was more fun to kiss,
But she raised up her dress when she spoke.

~~~~~

She married a fellow named Frick
Whose mouth had been switched with his prick.
    There was no sixty-nine
    But they got along fine
When they found ninety-six did the trick.

~~~~~

THE QUEER DOCTOR

To the doctor went poor Mrs. Potts;
The pain in her pussy hurt lots.
    Said old Doctor McLouth,
    "Let me look in your mouth,
For I'm fed up with looking at twats."

~~~~~

A man turned his head to the sky
And said, as a bird flew on high:
    "This manifestation
    Is God's great creation!"
But the bird dropped a turd in his eye.

~~~~~

When John fucked a girl from Purdue,
Tim would wait till his brother was through,
    Then Tim licked the paste
    For he relished the taste
Of a cunt where another man blew.

~~~~~

THE COPROLITE

Two diggers of fossils stood rapt
As wondrous new relics they mapped.
    Said one, " 'Pon my word,
    It's a fossilized turd
Where some creep in the crypt crept and crapped."

~~~~~~

The other man said as he stooped,
"I think that we both have been duped.
    No creep ever slipped
    And crapped in the crypt,
But a pup in the pit popped and pooped."

~~~~~~

When Kay left her boyfriend named Ray,
He looked high and low through the day.
    He got down on his knees
    And he begged his friends, "Please,
Let me know when and if you see Kay."

~~~~~~

As he entered the lift, Mr. Kropp
Was aroused and his pecker did pop.
    Through his fly, and was felt
    By a young lady svelte—
She went down as they rode to the top.

~~~~~~

DO IT FOR FUN

Give no help to poor people that roam
Seeking food as the alleys they comb.
    It is courting disaster
    For they multiply faster
And they'll fuck you right out of your home.

~~~~~~

COX SUCCORED

Young Cox, in despair, on the rocks,
Received aid from the parish *Poor Box*.
    Said the Pope, much impressed,
    "May this parish be blest
For providing the succor for Cox."

~~~~~

When Grover fucked old harlot Rose,
A problem she had to dispose,
    So she said to him, "Grover,
    I believe I'll turn over—
I can't stand the way you pick your nose."

~~~~~

CURE FOR HOMESICKNESS

A man far from home name of Russell
Engaged a young maid for a tussle.
    "I am homesick," he said,
    "So lay down as if dead,
And do not move a tit or a muscle."

~~~~~

To the doc went the whore of St. Anne's,
And her visit fit into his plans.
    He checked her cirrhosis
    By means of hypnosis,
Then he reamed out her twat with his glans.

~~~~~

The whore from the parish St. Giles
Retired amidst plaudits and smiles.
    When she figured each poke
    At three inches per stroke,
Her cunt had some ten thousand miles.

~~~~~

SAFETY PLAY

Said the young gynecologist Schick
As he probed in the crotch of a chick,
      "I am through, please relax,
      You can put on your slacks,
And you'd better let go of my prick."

The rooster, as well known in science,
Rules the barnyard by clucking defiance,
      Whereas lawyers in courts
      Are working at torts,
And their time is spent fucking de clients.

When problems arose, Mr. Scott
All day with great effort gave thought,
      But with simple precision
      He would make a decision
When he came face to face with a twat.

WHAT! NO HEADACHE?

When his wife passed away, Mr. Scott
Said a true-to-life posture he sought,
      So he laid her to rest
      With one hand 'cross her chest
And the other hand over her twat.

CHEESE DIP

The author proclaimed in his script
How man over kisses has flipped,
      But there's nothing so fine
      As the feeling divine
When the prick in the pussy is dipped.

There was a young lady named Sentry
Who claimed to be raped by some gentry.
    But the judge said, "Dismissed,"
    For he looked where she pissed
And saw no sign of forcible entry.

<hr />

When atom bombs fill up the sky,
You must give it the old college try.
    Say a prayer, if you please,
    Put your head 'tween your knees
And start kissing your asshole goodbye!

<hr />

STOCKBROKER'S ADVICE

Investment in sex would be sin,
Advised the old stockbroker, Flynn.
    If it's growth stock you hunt,
    Stay away from the cunt,
For you never get out what went in.

<hr />

There was an old harlot named Skillings
Who went to the dentist for fillings.
    In a fit of depravity
    He filled the wrong cavity,
So each cancelled the other one's billings.

<hr />

A destitute trapper was Skinner;
His catch was so poor he got thinner.
    He set off in pursuit
    Of the beaver hirsute
To provide him with warmth and a dinner.

<hr />

Great sculptors attired in smocks
Nude statues created from rocks,
But their names are forgotten—
We recall just the rotten
Old bishops who knocked off their cocks.

~~~~~~

Said the doctor, while checking Miss Sommer,
"Your urine may tell why you're glummer."
So she stooped to the floor
And she pissed like a whore.
"What you need," said the doc, "is a plumber."

~~~~~~

If your family is small, you will star,
And trips you can take, near and far.
It is not simple luck,
Just make sure you don't fuck
Yourself out of a seat in your car.

~~~~~~

On earth man has made a poor start;
In pollution he's put soul and heart,
But in Congress, their goal
Is to plug every hole—
Man will soon need a license to fart.

~~~~~~

A legless old lady of Strand
Was raped by a rotter named Rand,
But the judge set him free
For he said, "I can see
She has no leg on where she can stand."

~~~~~~

Astronomers sat with nerves taut,
Their telescopes trained on one spot
On the girl from Madras
For a view of her ass
And a total eclipse of her twat.

~~~~~~

OUT-OF-DATE WIRING
A man of his dear wife was tired;
It seems that her sex life expired,
So he switched her, at forty,
For two twenties, so sporty,
But he was for two-twenty not wired.

~~~~~~

While the chef was preparing a treat,
The waitress stood by so discreet.
When she asked, "What is love?"
He said, "Heavens above!
It is when I am basting my meat!"

~~~~~~

FLY THE FLAG
In the forest serene there grew one tree
Which had knotholes that made it a fun tree.
A lone ranger came by
And he unzipped his fly,
And said, "What can I do for my cunt tree?"

~~~~~~

PROPORTIONAL OBSCENITY
A learned old justice of Trent
Defined what obscenity meant.
He found *Duck* was not clean,
But three-quarters obscene,
And *Fudge* was foul forty percent.

~~~~~~

MUSH!

To Alaska went worn-out old Tucker
To gain back his strength as a trucker.
    He expended his wealth
    To recover his health
And he came back a strong husky fucker.

~~~~~~~

GAME TRY

The hunter of game, unobtrusive,
Prepared all his rifles exclusive
    To pursue the big cat
    In his wild habitat,
While his son stalked the pussy elusive.

~~~~~~~

FOR SHAME!

An ESP expert named Vance
Was walking the street, and by chance,
    When he read a girl's mind
    Was disgusted to find
That she'd like to get into his pants.

~~~~~~~

ARCHIMEDES PRINCIPLE

Archimedes while dipped to his waist
Tried to screw with a mermaid in haste,
    But he failed to account
    For his weight in his mount
Which did equal the water displaced.

~~~~~~~

REGIMEN FOR LONGEVITY

A maid who was trim but well-fed
Explained how her weight had been shed.
    Every night without fail
    Her intake she'd curtail
To a sausage and two eggs in bed.

~~~~~~~

There was a cheesemaker named Whithouse
Who lived in a fine and a fit house.
    To make limburger cheese
    For this man was a breeze.
He took two pails of milk to the shithouse.

~~~~~

THE FLYCATCHER
There was a young lady named Wise
Who claimed that her cunt ws a prize,
    And she fooled many men
    For they all came again,
But she never, but never fooled flies.

~~~~~

THE QUADRINITY?
Old Mary, it seems, has a yen
To play with a candle, not men.
    She'll be raised to the Trinity
    By the Blessed Divinity
If she shows she can do it again.

~~~~~

SINCOME TAX
To a whore said a tax man named Zend,
"On the sinful diversion you vend
    An assessment you'll pay."
    Said the whore, in dismay,
"You have syntax I don't comprehend."

~~~~~

GRAVITY OBSERVED
The schoolbooks with theories abound
How Newton had gravity found.
    Now it wasn't the apple
    Which his mind had to grapple
But the frolicking pair on the ground.

~~~~~

MAN THE INVENTOR

As new concepts began to accrue,
So with scarcity man was all through.
    He invented the lever
    And the wheel—no doubt clever—
But too bad he's in debt for the screw.

~~~~~

APPROPRIATE EMBLEM

As a symbol of note, we admit
The eagle is worthy and fit,
    But for principles narrow
    Much preferred is the sparrow
Who sings with great joy and eats shit.

~~~~~

There was a young fellow named Beakley
Who managed at first a tri-weekly,
    Then he tried with some care
    A try-weekly affair;
Before long he was doomed to try weakly.

~~~~~

THE RECTAL BALLPOINT PEN

To write a prescription, Doc Ben
Looked into his coat once again.
    When he found a thermometer
    He was heard a kilometer,
"Tell me what silly ass has my pen?"

~~~~~

VIRGINS IN THE FOREST

The ladies spend hours of bliss
In forests that hide every kiss,
    And no prying eye sees
    What occurs midst the trees,
So the forest's prime evil is this.

~~~~~

While driving, a fellow named Bonctor
Observed a young lady and honked her,
    But she failed to respond
    To this gay vagabond,
So he came and he saw and he conked her.

THE NUTHOUSE

When idiots by chance have been bred
They need to be cared for and fed.
    Though asylums are there
    It costs money for care,
So we send them to Congress instead.

A well-traveled lady of Crete
Was sunning herself with young Pete.
    He said, "Tell me, Irene,
    Why your back is so green."
She said, "Grass never grows 'neath my feet."

Said the hunter of game to Miss Granger,
"To the feeling of fear I'm no stranger.
    I respect the big cat
    In his wild habitat,
But a pussy that's small is no danger."

After fishing all day, Mr. Heldt
Was thrilled with the pride that he felt.
    He collected a catch
    That few anglers could match,
For two mermaids he caught, and one smelt.

A man should not search out a lay
At the place where he's earning his pay.
　　He should not get his honey
　　Where he's making his money,
And should not let his meat loaf all day.

～～～～

A fastidious old man of Alsace
Was fucking a girl on the grass,
　　When he noticed a sign:
　　"If you litter—pay fine,"
So he shoved his cigar up her ass.

～～～～

An old undertaker named Carriere
Prepared a cadaver to bury her.
　　They brought four more that night
　　And he cried in delight,
"The more that they bring in, the merrier!"

～～～～

A girl that smoked heavy had Chase;
Her breath stunk all over the place,
　　But her pussy smelled sweetly
　　So he kissed it discreetly
And he fucked her tobacco-stained face.

～～～～

A solemn gravedigger named Dave
Some remnants of dead whores did save.
　　He fucked with delight
　　The assemblage one night,
Though it still had one foot in the grave.

～～～～

In the winter a strumpet named Flo
Fell dead when a blizzard did blow.
    She was fucked by Count Rumford,
    But she gave him cold comfort—
She had lain for too long in the snow.

~~~~~~

THE BROWN-NOSER

To a pipe-smoking suckhole named Flock,
The death of his boss was a shock,
    So he chiseled a bowl
    From the corpse's asshole
And he fashioned a stem from his cock.

~~~~~~

SURROGATE SUBTERFUGE

An old undertaker named Flock
Once lifted a young lady's frock.
    She was fucked without strife
    For the time of her life,
But he fucked her with grandfather's cock.

~~~~~~

LONG LIVE NECROPHILIA!

On the night of the wedding, young Fred
Told his bride, before getting to bed,
    To please take a cold shower
    For at least half an hour,
Then to lie on the bed as if dead.

~~~~~~

When dead, an old harlot named Hayes
Received from devotees much praise.
    She was kept in behalf
    Of the coroner's staff,
For her pussy kept twitching for days.

~~~~~~

STILL, YET AND AGAIN

Said a man to a widow named Jill,
"Tell me, why don't you bury poor Bill?"
    She replied, "Though he's dead,
    I will keep him in bed.
He's my darling and I love him still."

~~~~~~~~

FLYSWATTER INCLUDED IN PRICE

To the madam went money-short Kyes;
His fifty-cent piece he thought wise,
    But felt something was queer
    When he patted her rear
And from out of her asshole flew flies.

~~~~~~~~

CAN'T LIVE WITH URNINGS

A henpecked old man of Lucerne
No peace in his life could discern.
    When his bitchy wife died
    He cremated her hide,
But he still heard her shouts from the urn.

~~~~~~~~

An arsonist hailing from Natchez
Was also a voyeur of snatches.
    To fulfil his desires
    To see snatches and fires
He ignited some snatches with matches.

~~~~~~~~

"What price for a whore, cheap and old?"
Requested a man without gold.
    Said the madam, "One buck,
    And it's not for the fuck,
But the scraper to scrape off the mold."

~~~~~~~~

THEREBY HANGS A TAIL

A wily old butcher named Pete Cook
Was fucking a whore with a beat look.
 She dropped dead with a twitch
 So he finished the bitch
As she hung by her ass on the meat hook.

~~~~~

SIMPLE INTEREST

A practical fellow named Prater
Wed a quad amputee of Decatur,
 And the poor girl was blind,
 But he said, "I do find
The percentage of twat is much greater."

~~~~~

THE LAST RIGHTS

In the hospital bed lay Miss Proctor,
Debauched by the rapist who socked her.
 As she cursed her abductor
 Seven orderlies fucked her,
And the interne, the priest and the doctor.

~~~~~

AN URN SAVED IS AN URN EARNED

The new wife of widower Raines
Caused nothing but misery and pains.
 She was not worth a durn—
 He got more from the urn
In which rested his late wife's remains.

~~~~~

DOWN IN FLAMES!

Young Moses, it seems, had a yearning
To pursue a strange method of learning.
 He ignited the hair
 Of a lady's affair,
And he talked to the bush that was burning.

~~~~~

Asked a girl of young astronaut Brad,
"What excitement in space have you had?"
    As he fondled her thigh
    He said, "Feelings run high
At the moment I lift off the pad."

For dinner the soldiers were clustered—
To a man they complained and they blustered.
    They accepted the soup
    Which was made of elk's poop,
But the moose turds were lacking in mustard.

A colostomy patient, Miss Clyde,
First despaired, then she took it in stride.
    She still peddled coition
    In the supine position,
But she made a lot more on the side.

WHEREVER THERE'S SMOKE ...
In the village the maids did conspire
With a monk who aroused their desire
    To send signals of smoke
    When they needed a poke—
Now wherever there's smoke there is friar.

A senile old hunter named Cotter
Observed a nude girl by the water.
    When he asked, "Are you game?"
    She said, yes, without shame,
So he raised up his rifle and shot her.

At the bird zoo, a man from Crimea
Said, "It seems like a brilliant idea
    To have all these birds dyed,
    But what bothers my pride—
How the devil does one dye a Rhea?"

~~~~~~

A lady well-bred and discreet
Was sucking a fire fighter's meat.
    It was not for the paste,
    But she relished the taste
Of the hickory smoked sausage treat.

~~~~~~

A Victorian young lady named Ewing
Had suppressed any passion for screwing,
    But one day, feeling chipper,
    She unzipped a man's zipper,
Which promoted a virgin's undoing.

~~~~~~

When we play at the politics game,
We kick out the scum that's to blame.
    Yes—the rascals are out—
    But it still leaves some doubt
For it seems that the stench is the same.

~~~~~~

A young lady depressed was Miss Glick
For her paycheck so small made her sick,
    Till she found a good way
    To mix pleasure with pay,
And a fly-by-night job did the trick.

~~~~~~

The buffalo hunter named Grange
Was courting a lady so strange,
    For he kissed what was hairy
    'Neath the stars on the prairie,
Then he fucked her at home on the range.

~~~~~~~

THE LONG RANGER

On the range, a young cowgirl named Granger
Was seduced by a copper-skinned stranger.
    It was Tonto, no less,
    But he lacked the finesse
Of the man in the mask—The Long Ranger.

~~~~~~~

LEAVE NO LEAF UNTURNED

In the Garden of Eden, in grief,
There sat Eve with a need for relief,
    Likewise Adam, so blue,
    Knowing not what to do—
It was time to turn over a leaf.

~~~~~~~

In the haystack a lady named Grimes
Recollected her fun in past times,
    But her quest inconclusive
    Found no needle elusive,
Though she did feel the prick several times.

~~~~~~~

Let us pity a fellow named Heep—
He was spurned by all harlots as cheap.
    Then the ultimate blow
    Which the Fates could bestow—
While he jacked off his hand fell asleep.

~~~~~~~

To her boss said a typist, Miss Hyatt,
"I am through—take a kite and go fly it,
  For I seek a transition
  To a better position."
Said her boss, "Please undress and let's try it."

~~~~~~

HOLEY CANDLES
At the abbey, the Cardinal knocked
And the Mother Superior was shocked.
  She had cause to suspect
  That he came to inspect
In the room where the candles were locked.

~~~~~~

ONCE A CORK SOAKER . . .
A young man who sacked coke in Fort Knox
Lost his job so he worked tucking socks.
  Then he moved to Grand Forks
  Where he tried soaking corks,
But he quit and he's now sucking cocks.

~~~~~~

A fag bumped a truck in Laporte
And the fender did slightly distort.
  Said the irate old trucker,
  "Suck my cock, you dumb fucker!"
And they settled the case out of court.

~~~~~~

Dear Abby advised every Miss
On the blessings of virginal bliss—
  Do not fondle man's meat,
  Keep his hands off your teat—
Cross your legs when he gives you a kiss.

~~~~~~

An old engineer name of Pete
Was giving a lady a treat.
    She could not understand
    What made fucking so grand,
So he showed her a sketch of his meat.

~~~~~~~

The sheep that I fucked last September
Within me has left a hot ember.
    Though I look every day
    I can't find the same lay;
Her vagina is hard to remember.

~~~~~~~

To heaven went Christ on his trip,
But someone had made a bad slip.
    From the cold earthly prison
    Of the tomb He had risen,
But the rabbi was left with a tip.

~~~~~~~

A thoughtful young widow, undaunted,
By her husband's demise she was haunted.
    The remains of her man
    She exposed to a fan,
For a blow job was what he had wanted.

~~~~~~~

A big-bosomed lady named Whipple
At Olympic events caused a ripple.
    She took on all competers
    In the one hundred meters,
And she beat the young lads by a nipple.

~~~~~~~

She challenged a sprinter named Jacques;
To distract him she raised up her smock.
>   But he moved out in front
>   When he glanced at her cunt,
And he won by the knob of his cock.

～～～

TOPOLOGY APOLOGY
The English prof eating Miss Young
Had thoughtlessly licked at her bung,
>   So he said, in apology,
>   "I know naught of topology—
Please exculpate this slip of the tongue."

～～～

RECALL
Her buttocks had started to chafe
In back of the car with young Shafe.
>   It did bruise and abrade her
>   And when this got to Nader
He declared all those models unsafe.

～～～

The priest told a lad to divest of it.
He said, "You must tell all the rest of it."
>   So the young lad did blurt
>   How he fucked Dirty Gert.
He felt good when he made a clean breast of it.

～～～

There was a young girl of Dundee
Who complained that she gave too much free.
>   Her beau felt a pang
>   When he heard her harangue;
He lay back and said, "This one's on me."

～～～

There was a young coed named Esther
Who claimed that the frosh could not best her,
    But a freshman, a jester,
    With his prick he did test her,
And he fucked her for one whole semester.

~~~~~

The noted Professor Herr Ewing
Gave coeds free lessons in screwing.
    "It's amazing," he said,
    "When they're stripped and in bed,
How so few of them know what they're doing."

~~~~~

An artful young fellow named Fred
Maneuvered his girl into bed.
    When she altered her mind
    It created no bind—
He maneuvered her mother instead.

~~~~~

The new secretary, Miss Gold,
Was fucking her boss young and bold.
    He was blowing his thing
    When the phone gave a ring,
So she put the young fellow on *Hold.*

~~~~~

A highly-strung lady named Proctor
Was checked by the doc who unfrocked her.
    He said, "You're in great shape."
    She said, "Don't stop, you ape!
It's a man I need now, not a doctor."

~~~~~

At the Firemen's Convention Miss Gump
Asked a fireman to give her a jump.
    Without thinking she chose
    A young man with a hose,
When she needed a man who could pump.

~~~~~~

With his finger, the able instructor
Directed a maid to conduct her
    To arrive home direct,
    But the route was suspect
For the finger was fickle and fucked her.

~~~~~~

GOOD THINKING!
To his wife said a fellow named Jay,
"Jump in bed and we'll have us a lay."
    Said his dear wife, distraught,
    "Though my head aches a lot,
I believe that my cunt is okay."

~~~~~~

On trial was a young man named Joe
For raping and beating Miss Flo,
    But the charge was dismissed
    For the proof did exist
She was beat when she failed to let go.

~~~~~~

There was an old man named Mahooty
Who found in a whorehouse a beauty,
    But his wife was a whore
    With a room right next door;
He was torn between love and his duty.

~~~~~~

When Joe came to visit young Nell
She convulsed in a bad, sickly spell,
    But she said to him, "Dear,
    There is nothing to fear,
For my grandmother fucks very well."

A devious young fellow was Neville,
Possessed of a bit of the devil.
    He screwed his girl Jill
    On the side of a hill,
Which proves he was not on the level.

In his car, a young lad of Purdue
A romance with his girl did pursue.
    He said, "Jump in the back."
    She replied, "No sir, Jack,
I would rather stay up front with you."

There was a young lady robust
Who thought that her date was a bust
    Till he slipped her his missile
    And her ass gave a whistle,
While the gas from his ass gave him thrust.

All evening the girl of young Shevor
Rejected his every endeavor.
    She made up with her lover
    But was sad to discover
That erections do not last forever.

A moral young lad who was trusting
Was stopped by a girl who was lusting
    For a man with a prick,
    So she dropped her pants quick,
But the hole thing, he said, was disgusting.

~~~~~~~~

A lady could not apprehend
Most sports where two people contend.
    She was much better at
    The game with the bat
Which dangles two balls at the end.

~~~~~~~~

There was a young lady named Brown
Who taught her vagina to clown.
    It could nibble a plumb
    And could chew Dentyne gum,
So her cunt was the freshest in town.

~~~~~~~~

A bride to be proud of, had Cole,
For he felt he achieved his life's goal,
    But he cried in despair
    When he viewed her crotch bare—
Someone ate it and left a big hole.

~~~~~~~~

On a date, the young girl will discover
Why the fireman is such a great lover,
    For the Lord only knows,
    When he reels out his hose,
How much time it will take to recover.

~~~~~~~~

To the doctor went itchy Miss Fern,
For the itch in her cunt caused concern.
    She was strapped with a cable
    To the hospital table
And the interns all fucked her in turn.

〜〜〜〜

A teacher of language, Miss Flock,
Had taught her vagina to talk,
    And it managed by rote
    An old biblical quote,
And could sing a few snatches by Bach.

〜〜〜〜

By hand, an old fellow named Fred,
Tried hard to erect it in bed.
    Said his wife to the fink,
    "I do really not think
You should flog an old horse that is dead."

〜〜〜〜

PUT UP OR SHUT UP
To his date, a young fellow named Hame
Said, "Your cunt is too big for this game."
    But she said, with derision,
    "It should fit with precision
If your prick is as big as you claim."

〜〜〜〜

There was a young woodsman named Kimber
Whose cock was so long and so limber
    That when brought to erection
    'Twas a work of perfection.
When it fell, all the ladies cried, "Timber!"

〜〜〜〜

There was a young man of Lapeer
Who said to his date, "You're a dear.
    Such a lovely big breast
    Would be fun when caressed."
So she gave him her blow-up brassiere.

~~~~~

Said the dentist to harlot McKay,
As he poked in her cunt with dismay,
    "Your life of depravity
    Has fucked up your cavity.
What you need is a gold crown inlay."

~~~~~

CASH CROP
A man saved old twats, if you please,
And he planted an acre of these.
    They grew up soft and hairy,
    Each one topped with a cherry,
And they all smelled like limburger cheese.

~~~~~

THE FOUNDRY CONNECTION
The widow of Baron von Rasting
Disclosed her devotion long lasting:
    "For a time I was sick
    As I missed his big prick,
But not now, since I made a bronze casting."

~~~~~

When you lay a young girl on the sod,
Don't consider the size of the prod.
    It's the way that you diddle
    In your ladyfriend's middle
That restores her relation with God.

~~~~~

THE ILLUSIONIST
Said the girl who was dating a swami,
"There are times I suspect that I'm balmy.
    There can be no dispute
    That his prick is minute,
But it feels like a full-size salami."

~~~~~

THE MAPMAKER
There was a topographer bold
Who fucked a fat lady, I'm told,
    And he mapped every cranny
    Which she had in her fanny,
And he fucked every wrinkle and fold.

~~~~~

RODEO
So wild was the lady of Bruce
They tied her ass down with a noose,
    Then a cowboy named Scott
    Shoved his cock in her twat
And proceeded to cut the bonds loose.

~~~~~

TAKE THE BOOK TO BED
From the sex book a fellow named Chris
Tried a stunt which his girl thought amiss,
    "I do not share your view—
    I have read the book too,
And the book was much better than this."

~~~~~

There were two old maids who were sisters,
And they never had dealings with misters.
    A repairman, undaunted,
    Gave them both what they wanted,
But first he replaced their resistors.

~~~~~

SHE HEARD HIM COMING

There was a young lady named Greer
Whose method of fucking was queer.
    If you asked for a whack
    At her front or her back,
She would smile and would turn a deaf ear.

———

To spice up his sex life, young John
Said, "Darling, new plans I have drawn.
    We will try it dog-fashion."
    But she said with face ashen,
"You will never get me on the lawn."

———

WITH THE FIRE HOSE

A spinster left burning with grief
Had been partially raped by a thief.
    By a matter of luck
    She observed a fire truck,
And the flame was put out by the chief.

———

"It's *Pony Express*," said Miss Pound,
"A sprightly new game that I've found—
    Like *Post Office*—instead
    You must play it in bed,
And there's also more horsing around."

———

FASTEN SEAT BELTS!

A vacationing lady named Violet
Took a plane to a far away islet.
    She slept sound in her seat
    And did not feel the meat
Of the captain, the steward and pilot.

———

The doctor, for old spinster Kieful,
Prescribed a young man for life gleeful.
    By the druggist 'twas filled
    And Miss Kieful was thrilled;
She came running right back for a refill.

As a man licked the asshole of Claire
She complained in a tone of despair,
    "Will you please try the cunt?"
    And he said, with affront,
"That's a bridge I will cross when I'm there."

There was a fellow named Crassus
Whose girl was the finest of lasses.
    Once he kissed her good-night
    And her legs closed so tight
That she fractured the frames on his glasses.

The pollution inspector, so droll,
Was eating a young lady's hole.
    He ran into a fart
    And he said, with a start,
"We must fix your emission control."

A determined old harlot named Gwen
Said success comes to those with the yen.
    If at first you proceed
    And you fail to suck seed,
Then by all means you suck, suck again.

A cocksucking lady named Koppers
Had chewed on some oversize whoppers.
    When she sampled the whang
    Of a fellow named Chang,
The fucking thing stuck in her choppers.

~~~~~

A cautious young lady named Liskers
Proclaimed that she only would risk hers
    For a man who was true.
    One man came—not to screw—
But he planted a kiss on her whiskers.

~~~~~

To Keith said a girl named McLouth,
"Be nice to us girls from the south,
    Or you'll get, my dear Keith,
    A crack in the teeth."
So he gave her a paste in the mouth.

~~~~~

A despairing young lady named Plum
Called a fellow and said, "I am glum.
    You don't come when I call."
    But he said, "Not at all,
If you blow the meat whistle, I'll come."

~~~~~

The doctor examined Miss Queen,
The dirtiest whore he had seen.
    He exclaimed, "I have not
    Seen so dirty a twat.
Hold still while I first lick it clean."

~~~~~

Said a fag to a queer named Salome,
"If you think you're so good, simply show me."
    Said the queer, "Why you prick, you,
    I will deck you and dick you
Long before you can throw me and blow me."

~~~~~~~

An old social worker named Shutes
Worked hard to assist prostitutes.
    He spent his last years
    With fairies and queers,
Enjoying the labors of fruits.

~~~~~~~

There was a young fellow named Thomas
Who said to his girl, "Let us calm us.
    When the times comes, we'll marry."
    But she was not too wary;
All she got was a lick and a promise.

~~~~~~~

A man with a girl named Carruther
Were sure that they'd love one another.
    She dated this Greek
    For a month and a week,
But he first threw the meat to her brother.

~~~~~~~

To the doctor went old lady Linkter
And he plunged up her asshole and dinked her.
    When she had a conniption
    He explained this prescription
Was not cheap, but was good for the sphincter.

~~~~~~~

A nun with a pious affinity
From priests took a course in divinity.
    They were fun to work under
    But it caused her to wonder
If that's how she lost her virginity.

The bishop who came from Berlin
Had a cock that was longer than sin.
    When he fucked his nun, Grace,
    It came out through her face
And it splattered all over his chin.

NOW WE KNOW!

The vilest of priests are collected,
Then bishops, archbishops selected.
    From the worst of this scum
    All the cardinals come,
And the Pope from the dregs is elected.

There was an old slut from the East,
A slovenly foul-smelling beast,
    And so utterly sordid
    That she'd never been boarded,
Except twice by the new parish priest.

Now what can a person expect
From people who think they're select,
    And who spend their time drumming
    Jesus Christ's second coming,
When the first one, you'll find, is suspect.

There once was a neophyte priest
Attending a holy day feast.
    In a trance he went forth
    With his asshole to north
While the nob of his dong pointed east.

~~~~~~

A man had his maiden agog
And was ready to slip her the log,
    But her dog interfered
    And a crisis appeared,
So he first threw some meat to the dog.

~~~~~~

The dog that we label first class
Is one that won't shit on the grass,
    And he will not be cursed
    If he licks your face first
Before licking his way through his ass.

~~~~~~

A fisherman queer name of Fife
Preferred screwing fish to his wife.
    Though he wrote a report
    On the fish-screwing sport,
He did not have a porpoise in life.

~~~~~~

MOTHER HUBBARD
For Bowser, a lady named Joan
Bent over to pick up a bone,
    But she met with disaster
    For her Bowser was faster,
And he had a big bone of his own.

~~~~~~

VIRGIN WOOL IS FASTER

If you want virgin wool, you must plan
And the flock you must carefully scan.
    Shear the sheep that are fleet
    Which are quick on their feet
And run faster than sheepherders can.

〜〜〜〜

In the pew the old Duchess of Corning
Let a fart without noises adorning.
    Said the bishop, with poise,
    "Please incorporate noise—
It would help if you gave me a warning."

〜〜〜〜